PONDERS II

Reflections

Susan Peters

Susan Peters
4- '10

authorHOUSE®

AuthorHouse™
1663 Liberty Drive, Suite 200
Bloomington, IN 47403
www.authorhouse.com
Phone: 1-800-839-8640

© 2010 Susan Peters. All rights reserved.

No part of this book may be reproduced, stored in a retrieval system, or transmitted by any means without the written permission of the author.

First published by AuthorHouse 3/16/2010

ISBN: 978-1-4490-7531-6 (e)
ISBN: 978-1-4490-7530-9 (sc)

Library of Congress Control Number: 2010902817

Printed in the United States of America
Bloomington, Indiana

This book is printed on acid-free paper.

This book is dedicated to the greatest of ponders…
our purpose for being.

"O Children Of Men!
 Know ye not why We created you all from the same dust? That no one should exalt himself over the other. Ponder at all times in your hearts how ye were created…"
 - from "The Hidden Words"
 - Bahá'u'lláh

…"O Thou Kind Lord! Unite all. Let the religions agree and make the nations one, so that they may see each other as one family and the whole earth as one home. May they all live together in perfect harmony…"
 -from a prayer of 'Abdul'-Bahá

Contents

In The Moment	1
Father Time	2
One Never Knows	3
St. Urho	4
Wonderments	6
Of Coffee	7
On Deeds	9
Serling-ish	11
Penguin?	12
Nature Astounds!	14
Morning Ode	15
Anew	16
So Many Boxes	17
An Amazement	18
And Counting	19
Tears And Laughter	20
Wee Hummer	22
Toward Understanding	23
Tapestry	24
"Mothers' Day"	25
More and Much	27
On Dreams	28
Not Far A-field	29
Given In Grace	31
Wonders Continue	32
Living Well	34
Life Change	36
"Fathers' Day"	37
CDL Fraud	39
On Diversity	41
Nature Symphony	43
On Pets	44
Not So Welcome	45
Fifty Two And Much To Do	47
Sir Hugh Beaver	48

Ode To A Face	50
"Grounded"	51
A Point Made	53
Percival	54
In Silence… Majestic	55
Oops	57
A Gift - In Point Of View	59
In Grace	60
On Adventure	61
Perk Server	63
If Only	65
Whatever	66
On Hope	68
Gifts Of Heaven	70
An Admiration	71
A New Pup	72
But Why?	73
Neurobic Brain Gym	75
Chosen Issues	77
Intangible	78
Getting On With It	79
Unexpected Inspiration	80
What On Earth?	81
Nature's Caress	83
On Blessings	84
On Confidence	85
Space Garbage	86
A Luminous Example	88
Faded Dreams	89
Ode To Those Long Wedded	91
Gold Facts	92
A Tidbit	93
To Begin	94
Mid-Life	95
Stilt Walker	96
Scientist Of The Year	97
Just How It Is	98

Toward Zero Tolerance	99
Endurance	100
Heart-warming	101
Lists	103
Crackdown?	105
Jason	106
"Gripper"	107
Realm Divine	108

In The Moment

We worry away so many moments
With thoughts of what might be.
How often do we find ourselves
Caught in past's reverie?

Fretting cannot change what is,
What was, or is to come.
On broken strings, "Oh woe is me!"
We may sit and strum.

Peace within cannot be known
With turmoil in the mind.
Just as we treat others,
To ourselves we need be kind.

So gently let us learn to clear
The clouds within our heads.
Let go resentments, all regrets,
Misgivings, fears and dreads.

Easier said than done, you say.
A challenge, yes, 'tis true.
But, one well worth the effort,
What better choice have you?

All that dwells within us
Affects all that we see.
One can play the victim,
But, by personal decree.

When past and future dominate
Our thoughts throughout the day,
We need to pause and realize
The present slips away.

Father Time

Well, Father Time has ushered in another year. Sure sneaks up on us, doesn't it? Despite the fact that each year consists of a fixed amount of days, weeks, months… it seems the calendar pages turn more swiftly and the time between the old and new ones has shortened. Turning eighteen, then twenty-one, seemed to take forever. Reaching fifty came so soon after thirty-eight, could a time warp have occurred?

Recently a dear friend from the past stopped by. Our visit was brief, but bursting with remembrances and reflections. Were either one of us where we'd once imagined we'd be? Had life so far transpired as our younger selves had planned? No.

Our lives appear to us as quilts. Some sections seem out of place in their fabric and texture, but those very same, that disrupt the pattern, have been strongly woven. The strengths of them, interspersed throughout, stand out and serve to bind the whole. No longer isolated at their specific points in time, they are seen differently now.

With the withering passage of time, if we so choose, our quilts provide for us a cloak of acceptance. Their weight is determined by how they are carried or worn. Mine rests lightly upon my shoulders, gently suspended by threads from above. In that there is a freedom: to observe, yet let go; to wander, yet remain rooted. In the moment a gentle acquiescence permeates perception of life's fabric; that of the past and all that it's been, that of the future and all it may hold; that of this new year as it unfolds. May we all weather it well, now more attentive to its fashioning.

One Never Knows

I am sitting near the fireplace, at a window, looking out at the Black River from a brand new house which is soon to be home. Unbelievable. Never would I ever have imagined it. Such is life; the unexpected comes to pass. One never knows.

It is wonderful to be detached from material things; to be able to delight in, but not depend upon them. This has always come easily for me, believing that we are but passing through, in this, our brief stay upon this earthly plane.

With free will we face trials, challenges, choices. Empires have risen and fallen to dust. Powerful leaders have ruled over kingdoms that exist no more; some majestic and bountiful, others oppressive and burdensome. It would seem then, that more importance lies in what we do and leave behind, in what is lasting… in how we live, rather than what we have or the things we hold to. There are no guarantees.

Oh, but surely this new home will be enjoyed. Such a bounty, such a blessing in the sharing of it. But, more so, it is one's loving heart and creative mind, an integrity in work and purpose, that embraces me in this moment. The houses are upon the earth for but awhile. That which brought this one into being, all that which is shared, will endure… as surely as a new day dawns.

St. Urho

Uplifted pitchfork in hand, displaying on end a skewered grasshopper (comparable in size to perhaps a turkey), stands Menahga, Minnesota's monumental tribute to a saint… of sorts. It is not the only such statue in existence, but the one I consider most noteworthy, as well as closest to home.

Although recognized officially in fifty states, and celebrated with his own holiday, March 16th (the day before St. Patrick's Day), he is unknown to most. Therefore, let me introduce you to Finland's patron saint, beloved of vineyard workers… St. Urho.

With but a pitchfork and the power of the Finnish tongue, this legendary pest controller eradicated hoards of locusts from Finland's grape crops. Ah, the grasshoppers no doubt froze with fright at his approach. Protective grape farmers, already dealing with a short growing season, had become desperate. Enter St. Urho, fork in hand: "Heinasirkka, heinasirkka, meine taatta hiiteen!" Rough translation: "Grasshopper, grasshopper, get the h--- out of here!"

In celebration of such a feat, the Finlanders yet applaud him, beginning with the day's rising sun. Woman and children gather at the lakeshore to chant as St. Urho did thousands of years before, in pre-Ice Age Finland. The local men folk gather as well. Dressed in costumes of green, they also chant, in addition to kicking aside grasshoppers as they walk down the hillsides toward the local lakes. Somewhere between the hilltops and the water, their costumes are changed from green to purple. Hmmm. That is perhaps the reason for their separation from the women and children.

Further research would need to be done, but a guess would attribute the costume colors to those of grapes. The Finnish-American festival began in the upper mid-west where many a Finn resides. As the Irish ethnic holiday, St. Patrick's Day, is dawning, St. Urho's Day has drawn to a close. The day's later hours had included a parade, the drinking of purple beer, the planting of donut seeds and the highlight of crowning another year's Grasshopper King.

On those last two, I shall leave you to ponder.

Wonderments

The capacity for wonder, a boundless ocean in childhood, seems to recede with the passage of time. There is no less to marvel at, to be curious of, to be amazed by. Perhaps, the naturally inquiring mind becomes stifled by the demands of the day, by worldly affairs. We are unaware that the sun is always shining. That simple thought adds magic to the moment.

The world turns. Darkness envelops us. There is no excitement at the dawning of a new day. We press the snooze button. While we are still able, we think not of those who can no longer hop out of bed. Rise and shine! There is a delight in that expression. Sad to say, it's been heard so often, the message no longer rings clear. O.K., although the sun is always shining, it is often blocked from view, especially this time of year. So, we may ask, "What bit of brightness can I bring to this day?" No one else has access to our personal dimmer switch. Sometimes it is most difficult to brighten our state of mind, to polish up the mirrors that reflect not only our outer selves, but our inner selves as well.

A most precious gift, the capacity for wonder, exists within us all. For many, it has shrunken, like the deflating balloons no longer bobbing about at the party's end. We simply pop them and throw them away. But, unlike the party balloons, our capacity for wonder can be re-inflated. Depending on the time and effort we are willing to invest, limitless expansion can occur. Wonderment balloons do not pop of their own accord. We pop them, deflate them, let go of them. Oftentimes, we simply let our expectations and disappointments diminish them.

As surely as the sun greets us each day, whether cloaked or stark naked in the marvelous sky, wonders abound. Beyond the clouds the sun burns brightly. Within us, may wonderments burn brightly as well.

Of Coffee

Coffee, a most popular beverage, had its start in Ethiopia more than 1,000 years ago. As far as we know, the first coffee shop appeared in Constantinople (present day Istanbul). It has been estimated that sometime between the tenth and sixth century A.D. an Ethiopian shepherd noticed that his goats became unusually frisky after munching on the fruit of certain trees.

Naturally curious, the shepherd and other members of his tribe eventually got to gnawing on the plentiful supply. The cherries were plucked from the trees, the pits mashed together and squeezed into baseball-sized balls. Yes, 'tis true. The coffee bean begins as a seed within the coffee cherry, which grows upon a tree. It was first consumed as a food, not a beverage. In Ethiopia the trees grew wild and human consumption was confined to that area for quite a lengthy period of time.

During the fifteenth century, the coffee cherry trees were obtained, planted and cultivated in southern Arabia; the land where appeared the Prophet of Islam, Muhammad; the land from which modern math and the zero were conceived. Then a repository as well of Greek and Roman contributions, the intellect ran wild. Turkish coffee was introduced. Not a quick brew was that; a combination of water, sugar and coffee patiently tended while brought to a boil, not once, not twice, but three times. Istanbul was home to that creation.

It wasn't until the 1600s that coffee was introduced to western Europe and England and coffee became connected with the Industrial Revolution. It was the drug of choice for the workaholic world. One could purchase, in London of 1652, a fresh, steaming cup for only a penny. It is said that the first ballot boxes appeared in London coffee houses; coffee houses that were associated with various trades and arts.

The largest supply of coffee beans to western culture were imported from Yemen. By 1658 the Dutch obtained seedlings. Paris began importing them as well in 1672. It was the French who spread the beans to Central and South America. In 1828 the magnificent beans sailed to Hawaii from Brazil. It was the Japanese immigrants who became Hawaii's coffee pioneers. One tree produces about a pound of coffee per year. That requires about 4,000 beans plucked from as many coffee cherries.

In San Francisco of 1881, the aroma alone of what was then exotic, was enough to gather customers to a small café. Eventually, national coffee giants were born: Hills Brothers, Folgers, Maxwell House and Yuban. Seventy-five percent of coffee volume was concentrated in but a handful of companies.

During the 1900s, the percolator pot became hot (pun intended), but was frowned upon by the coffee gourmet, as were re-heating and re-brewing. Price competition brought in lesser grades. No longer family controlled, quality declined. Coffee, a stimulant to the adrenal hormones, was soon thereafter classified within two categories: Arabica and Robusta… Arabica, of course, being of higher quality. Robusta blends, of lesser quality, were used in instant coffee brands. Their beans were more easily grown, resistant to diseases, had more caffeine and a bitterness, unpleasant to the serious coffee consumer.

The '50s witnessed a café boom in Italy and the rest of Europe. It was in Italy that cappuccino originated; a combination of espresso and steamed milk. In 1948 Milan entrepreneurs had perfected the commercial espresso machine. The secret was in the spring and pistons. Rapid force produced a superior extraction of coffee flavor.

By the late '50s and early '60s the coffee houses of California had become centers of intrigue, potent sources of ideas. Coffee was considered a stimulant to the imagination. For main stream folks, however, cheaper, quicker blends, off the store shelves, became the norm. What was considered necessary brewing time to the gourmet palette was deemed too slow by many for the increasing pace of life.

Well, so much for the beginnings of my favorite beverage. There is yet much to share of a history which began in the grazing land of goats, but we shall enjoy a bit of savoring ere that continues. Thank-you, oh informative cable channel, for a most interesting story to share.

On Deeds

"No good deed goes unpunished." These are surely not uplifting words to live by, but such is life that oftentimes…, well, let's just say that the path of good intentions is not without its briars and brambles. The source of this sentiment is unknown to me. It was quoted by my mother, at her kitchen table, over a cup of tea and a box of tissues. We chuckled. Her cold was departing. Mine had just made itself known. Dad was improving. Acute bronchitis he had.

My father had been a few days in the hospital when I headed north. I had just gotten over a nasty cold. Thank goodness I was better and able to go help out. Mom's cold hit the day of my arrival. Yeah! Dad's home from the hospital! Boo-hoo… mom's coughing and blowing her nose. My own bore witness to all the attention it had the past week and a half: dry, red, sore.

Several tests were scheduled for dad over the next four days. Between hospital and clinic we went. One day required two separate trips. Why they weren't done while he was an inpatient, we know not. As I chauffeured my dear ill parents around, did errands, talked with medical personal and helped establish a new routine (breathing treatments, exercises, etc.), it never occurred to me that I could become sick again… so soon. Nope. Not fair. Despite so much time spent with ill folks and visits to medical facilities where germs abound, it was unbelievable to me.

I remember saying once to a friend that it was most difficult to understand, to accept that a good deed, a favor, an act of love, of kindness, could be accompanied by any turbulence. If someone desires to do good for someone else, why can't it unfold smoothly, gently, an unsullied blessing? That was somewhat how the question was posed awhile back. "If I am here to help, why am I sick now?", I asked. Self-pity ran a short course, until memories of previous contemplations on the subject began to stir.

How much easier it would be, how puffed up one could become, if all one touched turned to gold, so to speak. With free will we have choices. Sometimes when things get tough, we back away. When gratitude enters in, wallowing cannot abide. The test, it would seem, is in the perseverance, and in attitude. Complaint or compassion? Ah, blessings do abound.

An intended few days in the U.P. stretched to more than a week. Again at home, it is much the same as shortly before the trip; tissue close at hand, no energy, sore and froggy-throated. But, may I always be willing to lend a hand, with acceptance of the unforeseen and awareness of the attending blessings. For in acceptance is a lightness of being. Sick and weary, wealthy and blessed am I. Such is life. Mom, dad, me… we did good. No good deed is warranteed. That I can accept.

Serling-ish

One frigid evening, wrapped in an afghan, I nestled into a cozy position and enjoyed a program on the Smithsonian Institution in Washington D.C. It was amazing. Although I've heard of it before, never was it realized just how massive and expansive it is; not only in its lay-out and number of museum buildings, but in content. A visit there is considered a cultural journey.

History, the arts, nature and wildlife are examined, as well as people and cultures, science and technology, and travel. Now, there's somewhere I'd like to go. Put that on the wish list. Remnants of the program flittered through my mind the following day. Again, to paper: Get "Smithsonian" magazine. Unbelievably, within days of watching the program, I received in the mail, correspondence from the Smithsonians, inviting me to become a member: a "Smithsonian National Associate". I read on. "Dear friend, thank-you so much for your recent visit… Which exhibit took your breath away?" I was thanked for my support. Hmmm.

Although it had been a rather rough year and forgetfulness is part of the mid-life transition, there is no doubt I'd remember having gone there. Could it be possible that the Smithsonian folks knew that a gal in Neillsville had watched the program, a visit via television? It was a "Twilight Zone" moment. Remember Rod Serling, narrating as we looked upon the puzzled expressions of unbelieving characters caught up in the unexplainable? Was I soon to be transported to another time, another place, a different dimension in time? How exciting! Flashes of "Twilight Zone" episodes came to mind, as well as the piercing look of Serling, so coolly unaffected as he invited us in.

Once the postage-paid card was mailed back, accepting the free Smithsonian membership and complimentary issue of their magazine, the day proceeded with no unusual occurrences. Disappointed? No. I look forward to the first of many visits to the museums via magazines that will open doors to things of which I am not aware. Marvels of the real world, inspiring to the mind, exciting to the imagination… doesn't get much better than that. Sorry Rod.

Penguin?

Once upon a time, when my daughter was a wee one, she brought up the subject of pets. The motherly pause button interrupted the stirring of pancake batter. Quick thinking and focus were required to soften the inevitable disappointment that would surely cloud her smiling face upon hearing that, in the apartment where we lived, animals were not allowed.

Continuing on with breakfast preparations, I asked, "Well, sweetie, if we could have a pet here, what kind of pet do you think you would like?" Images of playful kittens and rambunctious pups came to mind, as I expected a bit of conversation on one of the two.

Silence. She wore the expression of one awaiting another to open a special gift. Emphasizing her answer with expressive gestures, she announced, " I… would like…to have…a ….PENGUIN! Oh mom, they are SO cute!"

That is a precious memory. She accepted the fact, not only that penguins would not do well, nor be happy in our environment, but also that we would remain petless, at least for the time being. Around the corner of her acceptance however, was a most pleasant surprise. Within a matter of days it was discovered that fish were allowed. Off we went to choose one, along with the necessary equipment required to provide for its existence. A bottom feeder was later purchased to aid with maintenance of the aquarium and fulfill what my youngster deemed necessary companionship. A stuffed penguin was purchased as well.

Her fondness for penguins has continued to this day. Over the years, oh so many were to fill our home. Her favorites remain with her now, in her own. How that fondness developed is a mystery. Isn't it amazing how we're drawn to particular qualities of certain things? We can become fascinated with whatever, for reasons unknown. Trains, antiques, trolls… to each his own. For me, it's always been little things, literally. I am fascinated by the miniature, the tiny version of things. Why? I shall ponder that.

Nature Astounds!

Envision this: A lobster-like crustacean with a furry appearance. Filaments, resembling hair, possibly containing symbiotic bacteria, cover its extended claw arms. It is of pale color and has no eyes. This is not an idea for a science fiction piece. Such a creature has been recently discovered. It is but a mere six inches long.

Researchers, during an outing within a submersible vehicle on the floor of the South Pacific Ocean, came upon the wee fellow whilst studying hydro-thermal vents... 6,500 feet below the surface. "Yeti", so named by one of the discoverer/researchers, is now the first recorded of a new creature family: Kiwaidae. Ah, nature astounds! (Discover Magazine - The Year In Science - Jan. '07)

This is but one mention of the 100 top science stories of 2006. A photo of the little guy, or gal, is included, just opposite the page displaying a "super-ant".

The super-ant becomes airborne in a most unusual fashion, by biting against the ground. A latch on their heads is used to "prop apart their large, pincer-like mandibles". After tensing their muscles, the latch is released, creating a forceful acceleration. Up and away they go. Now, that is fascinating. They now hold first place in having "the fastest self-propelled strike in the animal kingdom", a position previously given to the snapping shrimp.

Well, two out of the hundred; has interest piqued? No doubt there will always be something new under the sun. There can be no disappointment for the enquiring, investigative mind when it comes to the natural world. Endless discoveries are yet to be made. We truly do know so little in relation to all that has been, is, and is yet to be.

Morning Ode

Ode to the morning, the dawning of days
The sun God has given, its life-giving rays
Wonders beheld as we welcome the light
After waking from sleep, from the darkness of night

In the quiet, the stillness, hope is enshrined
The spirit does beckon, "Be loving, be kind"
If listening intently, one may hear the cries
Against warfare and treachery, hatred and lies

For in the dawn's beauty a contrast is seen
When one's heart is at peace and one's focus is keen
In how the world is… and how it could be
Between lives out of tune and Divine Melody

Ode to the morning, beginning anew
A day to be lived and tomorrow not rue
Over words ill-spoken or virtues forsaken
Unseemly behavior or actions not taken

Each new day given in which we may thrive
Whatever our choices, for whatever we strive
May we be humble, keep our course true
Living life's moments from the dawn's point of view

Anew

We can look into the mirror on any given day, at any given moment actually, and start anew. The mirror isn't necessary, but provides emphasis, reflecting back to us an image. We look into our own eyes, past the hairdo, the concern for whiter, brighter teeth, the too dry or too oily skin… any trivial physical imperfections. We may gently and lovingly decide to be our own best friend.

This would seem a simple concept, but caught up in the details of daily living, we all too often set that aside. How important is it, when attention need be given to so much else, to indulge in a bit of quality time with our own self? Leisure activities, exercise, time for reflection, steps toward goals, ah… and connection with that which may lie dormant, awaiting to be re-ignited, stoked, or perhaps discovered.

We can surprise ourselves, just as we are surprised by others, in discovery of that which we were previously unaware. Outwardly we can tend many a garden. Inwardly we can tend but one; that which is uniquely our own. Each day is worthy of pondering, of reflecting on those things within ourselves that we can change, on the qualities we can graciously accept, and of all possibilities yet to unfold.

So Many Boxes

Upon moving, one realizes just how much stuff can actually be done without. It begins with the packing of that very first box. What do we put in it? Things we never use. Marked "misc.", it will no doubt sit among the other "misc." boxes in a corner of the basement for quite some time after the move is completed. You will later not be able to guess what is contained therein.

While surveying our new surroundings, often perched upon one such box, we are amazed at just how much has been accumulated over the years. While cleaning up the old place, emptied of all its previous contents, except for bare essentials, it dawned on me that there would be many, perfectly content to live there, just as it was. The appliances remain. The microwave, a couple of cups, plates, silverware, some toiletries. I paused to ponder wants versus needs, desirables versus essentials. A quote came to mind, but its author escaped me. Well, the quote was a bit hazy too, but the gist of it was that a person is rich in relation to the amount of things he can do without.

It is wondrous to be at peace, content in an empty room. It is a pleasure to fashion a room, a home, to suit one's tastes. It is a blessing to be where nature reminds us that our nest here is not permanent. All is more greatly appreciated if one can know serenity in an empty room, for all that may fill it is transient. What we see is much influenced by how we see it. In that, each day is a marvel, each space an experience in itself, an unopened box… contents unknown.

An Amazement

Out of an other-worldly, thick and chilling, eerie early morning fog it appeared. A dog perhaps? A wolf? No. The creature's pace was odd, erratic. It was not a deer. A tingling surge crept along my spine, settling in the tailbone. Focus was briefly interrupted as I contemplated the mystery of that particular sensation. Isn't it amazing how our bodies respond to visual stimuli, especially the unusual, the unexpected?

The form grew larger, its pace increased as it emerged from the most dense fog into a patchy area where its outline was but a wee more discernable. Still, nothing registered in the creature catalog of my mind. Bravely standing my ground, alone and unarmed, was I truly prepared to meet up with what could very well be an alien life form? It was, after all, emerging from a field. Field… crop circles.

As it drew nearer, the haze-engulfed body appeared ever larger, even more peculiar. The weirdness of this silent, early hour experience created apprehension, but not alarm. Patiently, tingling with anticipation, a deep breath was drawn as I faced the clearing into which the unknown would soon present itself.

What seemed to be an extended appendage, out of proportion to what followed, was bobbing along ahead, keeping beat with its stride. I was now totally fascinated, caught up in the moment and hoping nothing would disturb or startle it from its path.

The fog magically dissipated in the surrounding area, as if commanded to do so, or simply out of respect for the creature that now slowed its pace into the clearing and strutted past, completely ignoring me. No acknowledgement of my presence was given. I watched in awe. It was so amazing that I was not a bit disappointed in that it was an animal common to the area. What my eyes beheld was the grand-daddy of all turkeys. He was huge! Never, ever could I have imagined a turkey to grow so big. He's no doubt been around awhile and obviously felt completely at ease, strutting by as he did.

I was new to an area he'd strutted through perhaps a thousand times. He was established. I was a newcomer. Yup, he had silently announced his right of way. I can respect that. It was a moment to be remembered, and one that left an imprint, possibly to be recalled and applied somewhere down the road.

And Counting

Well, we've been at our new place for a couple of months now. This morning, while enjoying that first cup of java, mind tuned only to the wondrous variety of birdsong greeting the new day, a realization dawned: I've no idea how many steps lead down to the basement, nope, not a clue.

Now, this may seem to most not worthy of mention, but there are those who will relate to the impact of such a moment: the compulsive counter of things. The list is endless. As clothes are hung there is the counting of clothespins as each item is attached to the line. As the garden is watered, each plant receives a number. This action is more flexible, for it allows choice; the first, the closest plant, not necessarily number one. The pleasure of skipping about, whether in an alternating or random fashion is obtained, it seems, by a feeling of balance, fairness, and no doubt a sense of order… and control.

My father came upon me counting aloud, although quietly, in their kitchen one evening. "You do that too?", he asked. Hmmm. Could heredity play a part in such behavior? The counting of tiles, panels, designs in a pattern, etc., at times seems an odd thing to do, but not quite so odd as continuing to do so once the amount is already known. Is there some comfort obtained in the repetitive assurance of the unchanging, or a quivering anticipation of maybe arriving at a different digit? Who knows? "Who cares?", one might ask.

Well, yes, some ponderings are far weightier, more substantial than others. The point of this one is that, for those with the counting compulsion, there is hope. Such pattern of behavior can be broken. But, then again, now that I've realized that the number of steps is unknown to me… will I count them?

Tears And Laughter

Mother was quite moved by a most tender song, written and performed by John Denver. She wished for sister and I to hear it and discover somehow its title so she could purchase the CD. She popped in a VHS tape, on which had been recorded by friends, a concert shown on the A&E channel quite some time ago. The video contained many songs, but numerous breaks and commercials as well.

A beautiful song it was, in lyrics, melody and voice. It played through my mind, in and out, throughout the drive back home. To the Internet I went, and in but a short time, came upon "A Song For All Lovers", inspired by an elderly woman in Alaska, who had shared with Denver how she and her late husband of many years had loved to dance. How lovely. I wouldn't mind having that one myself.

Back to the video. It brought back many memories. I've not listened to Denver for years. Bittersweet those memories were. The first was of a concert attended in a high school auditorium in Kenosha, Wisconsin, back about 1970-71. It's hard to recall exactly when. The dear soul who treated me to that most enjoyable event, lived but only a few more years. There are those who've touched our lives, who will always be missed. It seems a part of us goes with them, or a least a space is left within, kept silent, but for those moments of reflection, often sparked by the simplest and most unexpected triggers.

A brief journey back in time ended as it was realized how much richer, powerful, controlled and soulful a voice had become over time. That voice remains for all who wish to hear it, although the man has left this life. Other voices from the past are left to the faltering memory.

Songs were sung on that video I'd not heard before, but most I had. With eyes closed, a wingless flight dipped in and out of the past, leaving a longing to hear a particular song that had been so uplifting after a long ago tragedy.

Guess it was time to get on with the present. Visits to the past are best as fleeting moments. Our minds would linger there if not directed back to the here and now, sometimes in a most peculiar fashion. This directive moment came in cathartic laughter, when bright as the sun bursting forth from the clouds, it was realized; the song I was waiting for, hoping to hear, would not be heard from this John Denver video, or any other for that matter… for it was done by Simon and Garfunkel.

Ah, yes. In the words of Kahlil Gibran, no doubt, in this life,… "forever tears and laughter".

Wee Hummer

Twice now have I had the pleasure of witnessing a hummingbird at rest, or rather, allowing itself a brief moment of stillness. The wee little creature pauses no longer than it takes for a simple sentence to be uttered. The feeder is mounted on a deck post within view of a favorite set-a-spell spot at the kitchen table and the tiny critter definitely notices me watching.

After feasting on the nectar, in a now familiar spot, he comes right to the window and performs. One cannot but sit in awe at the miniature acrobatics and wonder at how, between acts, he remains suspended, motionless but for those delicate, tireless wings.

Energy from what has been consumed, already expended, he returns to the feeder's bright red nourishment. Although the many feeder holes give access to but one entrée, he makes of it a smorgasbord by first hovering over, then partaking of, each one. Again he returns to the window. I believe he is thanking me. Then, off he goes. The ability to follow would no doubt lead to quite the adventure.

What he has received has been returned many times over. Without words, without touch, leaving nothing tangible behind, precious moments of being linger. A heart has been touched. The hummingbird will return and experiencing such presence will never grow old.

Toward Understanding

How many children stare at themselves in the mirror, wondering why both sides of their faces are not the same? While others are debating over whether the UFO in the sky is a bird, a plane, or Superman, some just stand aside in awe over how whatever it is stays up there in the first place. I was such a child.

While growing up, three brothers and I (before sis was born) alternated between Lutheran and Roman Catholic church services; a short distance from each other, one Sunday with mom, the next with dad. How different they were (the services). It left me wondering, way back then, which church God was at on each particular Sunday. How odd it then seemed, to be more intently aware of an Almighty Creator while sitting high up in a tree, or alone in a room. Occasionally, obsessing over such things would occur; never were they just blown off, but most often they just faded out for a time, and gently reappeared in the stream of thoughts further along.

While an art major at a Wisconsin university a favorite professor announced one day, while having us stare at ourselves in mirrors, that each side of the face has its uniqueness. They are not the same. Hmmm. As for large, heavy airborne objects, the mechanics of that still elude me and lead to brain strain, although the concepts of kites in the wind and critters with wings has been grasped.

Over time we begin to understand many things. Some things are never really understood. But, we may ponder them nonetheless. Back to being high up in that tree; that has been the mightiest, continuing ponder of all, an enduring one which has been most fruitful. Many years of reflection, comparative studies and the blessing of visiting the Holy Land, so rich in religious history, has rooted me in the belief that there is but One Reality, One Fashioner of all.

I believe that it is in our perceptions of Revealed Truth, given through different Mouthpieces over time (the Founders at the core of the world's existing faiths), that differences have arisen. It would seem then, that acceptance of a pervasive unity, in diversity, would reveal a common ground. If one is color blind, unable to discern green from blue, the truth of colors remains the same. The importance of substance outweighs that of perception, for perceptions are subject to change.

Tapestry

A dear friend shared an article with me last week, from a paper she very much enjoys, "The Tapestry". The article had to do with individual destinies and how, throughout our lives, not only in spite of our struggles, woes and misfortunes, but due to them, glimmers of guidance are given. We may later become aware, with the passing of time, that pearls have laid hidden within our sea-beaten shells.

If one were to make a list of one's sorrows, those scars of experiences and memories we all carry and bemoan, a determined objectivity may reveal that another list exists which contains most, if not all, of the same. That other list reflects to us what we have become, what we have endured, where we are heading, how resilient and strong we truly are.

The woes of depletion may lead to realizations of potential. Within the void of our losses, our pain, exist the buds of possibilities, dust-covered pearls, life-giving waters, but we see emerging from the depths of darkness only weeds, stones, murky streams. Some carry such visions throughout a lifetime. For some, the mourning never ceases. For others, new mornings dawn.

Faith, shifts in perspective, and acceptance are but a few of the keys to the opening of new doors, the dispellers of dark clouds. Life, seen as a mighty river, continues to flow. We can release our grip on the unstable branches to which we cling along the river's edge, and continue on. Every river has its bends. We can let go and move on.

"Mothers' Day"

"A printed card means nothing except that you are too lazy to write to the woman who has done more for you than anyone in the world. And candy! You take a box to Mother - and then eat most of it yourself. A pretty sentiment!" -- Anna Jarvis

Anna Jarvis, a Philadelphia spinster, gave birth to an American enterprise which she later waged war upon. As a gift to her own departed mother (1905), Jarvis, an insurance clerk, set out determined to make of her mother's dream a reality. Beginning in 1907, with the financial support of department store tycoon, John Wanamaker, Jarvis spent the next seven years on a promotional campaign to establish a nationally acknowledged holiday for moms. Success was achieved in 1914, when Congress, under President Woodrow Wilson, passed a resolution for "Mothers' Day". Mission accomplished, no doubt she was pleased… for some years.

By 1923 Jarvis was appalled that "…the charlatans, bandits, pirates, racketeers, kidnappers and other termites… would undermine with their greed, one of the finest, noblest and truest movements and celebrations." A new campaign began, for "Mothers' Day" was not intended to be a source of commercial profit.

Over the next twenty years Jarvis lectured and battled against violations of her copy-righted term,

"Mothers' Day", the increased cost of carnations (the official "Mothers' Day" flower), and the claim put forth by the Society of American War Mothers that a man had actually initiated the holiday. She was greatly displeased with Eleanor Roosevelt endorsing a "Mothers' Day" tribute, as well as with Franklin D. Roosevelt's design, and the post office's promotion of a commemorative stamp.

For fifteen of those years Jarvis secluded herself within a three-story house, opening the door only to those informed of a secret knock. She then spent the remainder of her days, 1943-1948 (age 79-84), partially deaf, blind and broke in a sanitarium, where ironically, some of her bills were paid by a trade association: The Florists' Exchange, and not a mom herself, receiving thousands of "Mothers' Day" cards each May.

Rather a sad story, that of Anna Jarvis. It would seem befitting for her to have an annual celebration day herself. One would think that the instigator of such an enterprising American venture would've received quite the slice of the "Mothers' Day" pie, though it appears she'd have no part in that. Or at least she may have been given some say in how such a holiday might be observed.

So, on this "Mothers' Day", let us remember the woman who put "Mothers' Day" on the calendar, as well as her intentions for that day's meaning. Let us ponder that... what would really please mom, with or without the flowers, the dinner, the candies and chocolates? Oh yes, and the card.

This information was obtained in an article by Marshall S. Berdan, entitled, "Change of Heart".

P.S.
"Mothers' Day" ranks #1 for long-distance phone calls
#1 for eating out, and
  #3 for the sending of greeting cards.

More and Much

Mega, ultra, max… double, triple, super. Where do we go from there? When does more become too much, or wasteful? Super-sizing has taken its toll; more than half of the American population now registers as overweight or obese. Then there are those battling eating disorders. Some too much. Some too little.

On a lighter note, consider toilet paper. Double rolls have led to jumbo rolls, then to jumbo double rolls. An extended roller is provided with the purchase. Being the creatures of habit that we are, do we really use less, or do we stick to the length we have grown accustomed to pulling from the roll? Are we flushing the bonus? Pleasing the plumber? Also going down the drain, perhaps… our savings on concentrated dish soaps and shampoos. While waiting for the billowing suds to dissipate, the dishpan water grows cold. Years of giving a good squirt into the running water has put us on auto-pilot. Who stops to think, "O.K., just a dribble will do."?

As for the concentrated shampoo; I've on numerous occasions had no need of anything else in the shower stall. Once again… habit. Economy-sized bargain brands for a growing family of seven, then years of thrifty sensibility on a low-income budget, led to total amazement at the dollop-will-do hair cleansers. Only once have I followed those directions. I kid you not. The very first time was a focused trial. I believed it not, so testing was required. Yup, very little did the job. After the proof, no further attention was given. Hence, a hair wash has become a standing bubble bath. I'd put a waterproof post-it-note in the shower stall, but wouldn't be able to read it without my glasses.

On Dreams

"…to find a dream and a life of their own…" This is but one line from just one of the innumerable songs referring to dreams; not those dreams which occur while sleeping, but dreams as related to desires, wishful thinking, aspirations, the fulfillment of romantic love, etc. There are far less songs sung of our sleep time visions, dreams that occur without pondering or intent.

Assuming that dreams, like so much of outstanding verse, literature and artwork, abound in symbolism, it would seem a realm of richness… the world of dreams. Aside from nightmares, with their various causes, or those bizarre, nonsensical sleep-time adventures which some attribute to food or drink, dreams may lead to the opening of doors, creative sparks, new understandings. Events may occur in one's life that seem to have occurred before (déjà vu). Perhaps a previous dreamland experience has come to pass in the physical realm. Who's to say?

In dreams we travel. Emotions are felt. We touch, we hear, we see; all as the physical self needfully rests for another day. How wondrous the workings of the mind! How incredible the bounties bestowed upon the spirit of man! And us gals as well, of course.

Not Far A-field

When thinking on the unearthing of treasures and traces of ancient times, thoughts and images drift throughout far-off lands. Major excavations, archeological digs, hunts for precious gems occur in desert lands, shrouded in mystery, where mirages baffle and camels plod, do they not? Well, that realm of contemplation has truly been expanded; not farther-reaching, but closer to home.

In our neck of the woods, remnants of ancient times have most often turned up by chance. Here in Wisconsin, discoveries have occurred as ditches were dug and roads were constructed. In the 1930s quite a discovery was made, in Kenosha County. After a period of local interest and curiosity, the findings were boxed away. During a holdings' inventory of Kenosha County's Historical Society… "Now, where is that box of bones?" Ah, turn up they did, in the dusty basement: mammoth bones.

Now, by the 1990s, mammoth bones were no longer a rare find in the area, but it was discovered that these particular bones were a rare find indeed, for they displayed cut marks made by human hands, most likely from butchering.

Needless to say, purposeful excavating ensued. In the summer of 1992 a site was chosen. It wasn't difficult to decide on, for the only exact location known was determined by an existing sketch, done after an accidental find in 1964. The dig was hugely successful. Bones were found, stacked in a pile, not scattered about. Beneath the pile of bones, which also bore cut marks, were tools of stone.

To the surprise of all involved, after radiocarbon dating was done, the bones were found to be approximately 12,500 years old. That did not jive with what was believed to be the earliest appearance of humans on the American continent. Eventually, bones were unearthed at other sites.

Much has changed since I left Kenosha, where I lived for many years. Longing to reside in a smaller town, the north beckoned. Folks down that way have long said I'd not recognize the once familiar city, which has become quite the Wisconsin metropolis.

Dig a basement, dig a trench, the odds are good that something will turn up. The Kenosha Public Museum now has on display a 95% reconstructed mammoth skeleton. Mastodons, referred to as the mammoths' cousins, have also emerged from Wisconsin's soils, as well as giant beavers. How big were they, I wonder?

Given In Grace

I caught myself smiling one dark, dreary day
While feeling the blues might just be here to stay
Battling depression, familiar with gloom
Those stretches of time, which for joy leave no room
Rising above, often carried with prayer
In the darkest of moments, wrapped still in God's care

I caught myself smiling, much to my surprise
The realization brought tears to my eyes
For having grown weary, with patience threadbare
A break in the clouds showed the sun was still there
With no rhyme or reason, one's chemistry shifts
Despite all the blessings and life's many gifts

I caught myself smiling, a brief span of time
Yet enough to remind me of the pure and sublime
Given in Grace, for to carry me through
I caught myself smiling, for the gift that is you

Wonders Continue

The coffee pot was finishing up its auto-process. I never seem to hang in there until the final gurgle. Thank goodness for that pause and serve feature. A fresh half-cup (rationing these days) with a sploosh of 2% (half & half is history) accompanied me to my early morning perch at the east corner windows, which then open to the dawn breezes, not yet carrying the heat of the day. It is 5:00 a.m. Some may think, "O.K., the sun rises, the birds sing, a deer or two, maybe more pass by." Perhaps. Ah, but so much more! There are always variants in the dawning of days.

One morning a wee hummingbird appeared. Its arrival was so startlingly quick, it seemed to have burst into creation just inches from the window pane. Hovering messenger of joy; so tiny a creature, so vast its aura of delight. A woodchuck waddles into view, not always from the same direction. It emerges from the trees, but prefers to take the recently placed steps down to the river. Its behind bidding good-bye, it disappears over the embankment. I've not yet seen it come up the stairs.

On this particular morning, eyes were drawn to a form atop a distant flagpole. An eagle, I thought; not yet "bald", perhaps a couple of years old. But, no. Focusing in, the binoculars delivered not the expected. An owl it was, perched upon the pole top like a king upon a throne, surveying the kingdom. Head to left. Head to right. Motionless body. Head to left. Head to right. Oh, come on! Turn around Let's see that face.

Viewing its backside, marveling at the size and its patient surveillance, I was soon to be stunned, for I'd forgotten the owl's remarkable ability. With a head-turn to the left, head continued to turn… half-circle, 180 degrees, yes? Directly at me, now he gazed. Rather hypnotic. A silent interchange ensued: "Bet you can't do that."

"Well, that would be a definite, 'no'. Nor could I perch upon a flagpole."

"Hmmm. Pardon me… scanning for morsels."

It was to myself alone I commented on its regal appearance and incredible patience, as I sat in nightshirt, hair un-brushed, wanting more coffee. In the blink of an eye, apparently a morsel had been spotted. Not only did the flagpole stand, no longer graced by the majestic owl's presence, but the creature itself was nowhere to be seen. The disappearance was as sudden and unexpected as the hummingbird's appearance had been.

Maybe tomorrow I'll spruce up a bit before settling in at the window. While the coffee is brewing a practice in patience could occur. Maybe I too could surprise someone with a gift of the unexpected. Such a joy, the senses. So rich are we in moments of observing, listening. How precious those moments of reflection, so often inspired by the unexpected. Rays of this day's sun begin to caress the distant trees. Already the breeze has grown heavier; heat and moisture building up for what's to be perhaps a record setting day in temperature and accompanying humidity. The windows close. The wonders continue. Such are the thoughts of a particular morning.

Living Well

A friend and I chatted as we put on our street shoes after our committed slot of morning time spent at the "Living Well Health and Fitness Center". Neither of us had felt quite up to it, but together the "force" was with us and the nearly aborted mission was accomplished. Happy were two hearts, like children after recess, refreshed to return to the pace of the classroom.

Other muscles respond differently. An adjustment period is required as they become accustomed to repetitive motion and weights, again like children, often resistant, yet later calling out, "Look what I did!" Balance is sought by each and every soul, although often we remain unaware of that need: for body, for mind, for spirit. Harmony is sought, from within each individual, for humanity as a whole. Ah, the greatest of contemplations… harmony, unity, and the attainment thereof.

As for the mind, I wished to share with my friend a few excerpts from a recently discovered (garage sale purchase) book: "You Are Not Alone: 1,000 Unforgettable Moments… Of Which We Could Remember Only 246", by Tom…uh… Friedman. Having read many, I shared but those few recalled at the time. Sharing of lapses in memory of the greatest of minds may serve to lighten responses for those of us of a more average mental capacity.

1) "Photographer Ernst Haas took a famous picture of Albert Einstein, which shows the great physicist thoughtfully rubbing his chin, as if he were pondering the mysteries of the universe. In fact, the picture was taken right after Haas asked Einstein where on the shelf he had put a particular book."

2) "A friend of Ludwig van Beethoven's named Frederick Stark called on him one morning and found the great but forgetful composer in his bedroom, getting dressed. Curiously, Beethoven's face was covered with a thick layer of dried soap. He had lathered his face the night before, planning to shave, then forgot to do so and went to bed."

3) "Columbia University philosopher Irwin Edman once visited the home of a colleague. At 2:00 a.m. Edman's colleague began to yawn pointedly. When Edman didn't take the hint, the man said, 'Irwin, I hate to put you out, but I have a 9:00 class tomorrow morning.' 'Good Lord!, Irwin replied, 'I thought you were in MY house!'"

Well, now time for some refreshment of spirit… after a return to "Living Well" to retrieve my purse.

Life Change

This has been the first summer in over 28 years that I've not been bronzed by the sun. There are no shorts, sandals, dresses, or other such seasonal wear in the closet. Free-spirited gadding about, enjoyment of garage sales, gardening and landscaping; any daytime outdoor activities... now avoided, or if absolutely necessary, stressfully endured. Retrieving mail from the roadside box can wait until nightfall, unless it's raining, gusty or cold. For the first time ever will Winter be welcome.

Stinging insects, having their part in the natural world, have always been accepted, respected, even marveled at, actually. Never, even after many times being stung, has their existence prevented, or hindered any project, plan or purpose... until, at mid-life, an allergic reaction occurred.

Am I saddened by this? Of course. Have I over-reacted? Perhaps, but the over-abundance of such creatures this year, as well as the far-above-average number of folks who have this year been stung, while just minding their own business, has surely magnified what has become a threat to me.

Do I intend to spend the remaining summers of this life within a sheltered space? Absolutely not. I see acceptance of this lifestyle change as a process, needful of patience; an adjustment over time. The inevitable internal screaming of, "Why me?!", was short-lived. "Poor me" is not a productive nor a pleasant state of mind. There are far worse bumps in the road of life. There are far greater challenges in this life's journey. And always, there are gifts and lessons in all that comes to pass.

We've so often heard the expression of how when doors close, others open. Perhaps not as quickly as we might hope for. Hmmm. When "Woe is me" weighs heavy and doors seem closed all around, it may take a mighty effort to arise and try those doors. Oh yes, and remember... the windows.

"Fathers' Day"

It was in the state of Washington, 1909-1910, that the idea for "Fathers' Day" was proposed. In the city of Spokane, initiated by a Mrs. Sonora Smart Dodd, supported by the local Ministerial Association and YMCA, it was established and first observed on June 19th, 1910 and soon spread throughout the United States.

Woodrow Wilson was President in 1914 when Congress passed a resolution for "Mothers' Day". In 1916 "Fathers' Day" was observed by him and his family. He later wrote to governors across the country, stating that its observance could, "establish more intimate relations between fathers and their children" and would "also impress upon fathers the full measure of their obligations."

In 1924 "Fathers' Day" was supported by President Calvin Coolidge as a nationally recognized tradition. Official recognition was sought by many. After all, "Mothers' Day" had been designated as a national day of remembrance for moms. Senator Margaret Chase Smith, in 1957, wrote to Congress of her sentiments on the subject: "Either we honor both our parents, mother and father, or let us desist from honoring either." She felt that to omit one was "a most grievous insult." Such feelings were shared by William Bryan, an orator and political leader, as well. In 1926 a National "Fathers' Day" Committee was formed in New York City. It wasn't until 1972, sixty years after its proposal, that "Fathers' Day" was officially established, although it had long been acknowledged and celebrated. Both Presidents, Richard Nixon and Lyndon Johnson, had a hand in that.

It was Johnson who proclaimed the third Sunday in June as the official observance day. As with "Mothers' Day", initially proposed by a daughter's wishing to honor her mother's dream for all mothers,

"Fathers' Day" began with a daughter's wish to honor her dad. On a Sunday at their church, while listening to the sermon on the honoring of mothers (the campaign towards establishing "Mothers' Day"

was ongoing, to be accomplished approximately four years later), Mrs. Dodd reflected on her dear father, his sacrifices, dedication and commitment to his children. A single parent, Civil War veteran and farmer, he had raised six children; Sonora and her five brothers. The wife and mother had died after giving birth to their last child.

The first "Fathers' Day" celebration, June 19th of 1910, was also the birthday of the man who had inspired its establishment, Mrs. Dodd's father, William Jackson Smart. The rose was chosen for the "Fathers' Day" flower: red for fathers living, white for those deceased. "Fathers' Day" ranks number five on the American greeting card-sending list.

CDL Fraud

Interstate trucking firms in the United States have grown from 20,000 to 564,000 since 1980. Two results of that growth are obvious: A massive increase in the number of semis and other large trucks on the highways, and an ever greater increase in the need for qualified drivers. It has been estimated that there are 1.5 million such vehicles on our roads throughout the country at any given time. What is not so obvious is a most alarming reality, which centers around the operators of those trucks.

More than a regular valid driver's license is required to operate commercial trucks. Particular skills are necessary, which must be mastered. These drivers must be certified and obtain commercial driver's licenses (CDLS). Safety advocates have determined that tens of thousands sham-licensed truckers drive our highways.

CDL fraud cases have been reported in 32 states. According to a 2006 U.S. Dept. of Transportation (DOT) report, following an investigation of approximately 15,000 "suspect" drivers in 27 states, one-third of them are no longer in possession of their bogus CDLS. Fraudulent licenses are obtained in a number of ways. Certification and answers to written tests can be bought through state-controlled companies for anywhere between $500-$1500+. False documents can be prepared. Exam answers are provided by translators to non-English speaking applicants. Truck driving schools have actually paid testers to pass those who have failed. After discovering such a practice (a case in Macon, Georgia), where third party testers were paid by a trucking school to pass some failed tests of 623 students, state officials required the tests to be retaken. Of the 623 students, only 142 passed.

In many cases, those we trust to protect us are involved. Some states' officials have sold fake CDLS, by the hundreds, to non-English speaking immigrants who didn't even make it through the pylons driving test, unable to maneuver through and around them.

Not only are the necessary skills absent in so many behind big-rig wheels, but important radio warnings from other truckers go unheeded by those who cannot understand them. There is no national CDL records database. There are only eleven states that notify trucking companies of violations by their drivers. Citations are slow to be entered into state

DMV computers. When a violation occurs in one state by a driver licensed in another, a violation may lag far behind.

Specific incidents involving truckers with invalid licenses are too awful for me to write of. Accidents happen even to the most cautious of us average drivers. The interstate trucking business, generally speaking, is yet another broken system in need of repair, an urgent issue indeed. For more information on this subject:

Michael Crowley at outrageous@rd.com. This information was obtained from an article published in the July, 2007 issue of Reader's Digest.

On Diversity

We marvel at the astounding number of animal species on our planet and their particular characteristics. Drawn more to some than others, we are nevertheless left in amazement of all, if we consider them for more than a few moments.

We notice, always, nature's many colors. Autumn especially engages many in travel, just for the sake of seeking out and admiring the most intense displays. There is no simply red, orange, or yellow. There is no simply green. In green alone exists a palette all its own, as well as one which shares a bit, here and there, from others.

Variety is said to be the spice of life. We surely do appreciate that in a culinary sense. Few are satisfied with simple sameness with our foods, except of course, those who have not tasted of the smorgasbord of choice, those whose meager fare does no more than take the edge off daily hunger, those who know not of cuisines and indulgences.

The pleasant and adorable are attractive. The familiar is comfortable. What we believe to know and understand frames our little worlds, which may expand, through curiosity, interest, necessity, caring. Such a variety in the animal kingdom, in geography, in nature's abundance, in our own gardens… we acknowledge them, appreciate them, wonder at them. Yet so many of us, human beings, treat and look down upon others of the human species as members of a lesser sub-group. Prejudices, born of ignorance, as well as a lacking humility, are reinforced by isolated, limited, negative exposures which magnify and create the view of stereotypical "others".

The wonders of the animal kingdom exist, first and foremost, in its magnificent variety. Ongoing discoveries continue. No doubt there exist still, creatures yet unknown. The awe-inspiring magnificence of the natural world, with all its contrasts, is made more beautiful. Landscapes, gardens, delight the senses; flowers, trees, even weeds… so different in color, fragrance and form.

Would it not seem within the natural order of things, given that mankind is of one species, that such diversity would be cause for celebration? Most of us, in this country alone, are a mixture, a combination package. I am an American. Hmmm: Finnish, German, Hungarian, Dutch and Cherokee. The garden of humanity is a plethora of blooms. With all our differences, whatever they may be, we are as one, unitedly, human beings.

Nature Symphony

The trees were dancing, each to its own melody
Seen as a whole: a visual symphony, directed by the wind
The tall grasses seemed to flow, like waves, surging towards the river
Currents of green, giving the illusion of buoyancy
Led to thoughts of floating among them… a verdant ocean

Tumultuous clouds changed form so swiftly
No single image could be discerned
So unlike those billowing whites
Their morphing displays, distinct against an azure sky

The birds competed, so it seemed
In bracing against Nature's gusty breaths
Wee acrobats, calling out in their variety of twitters
Not unlike young children in the enjoyment of carnival rides

All too soon came stillness: a brief, silent vacuum of time
The rain began, not as expected; no storm's torrent of pelting sheets
The clouds, no longer raging, had simply melded together
Their various hues united, now a silvery mass
Which gently delivered its life-sustaining waters to the earth

On Pets

Our precious canine will be four years old this month. He is a Peek-a-poo (Pekinese/Poodle mix) we named Hansomman. Most often we just call him Shrimp. Neither makes the top ten list of the most common dog names, which appears on the Tribune pets blog. Good.

Names for both dogs and cats are listed, chosen from among 450,000 insured clients, according to Veterinary Pet Insurance. Believe it or not, the number one name for both dogs and cats is Max. It was a surprise not to find Lucky on the list, for Luckys many have I met.

Sister has a cat named Baxter (not on the list). Dear friends have a dog named Sundance (also not listed). This is a good thing, uncommon, rather special, don't you think? This topic brought to mind my mother's mention of a childhood pet. Its name I do remember. How that name came about… not a clue. Her Finlander farm family named their dog (spelling it as it sounds) Gobushgooshkee. Now, that's worth looking into. Now added to my ever-present list: Ask mom about dog.

Here are the rest of the most common names for the insured canine and feline population:

Dogs… 2-Molly, 3-Buddy, 4-Bella, 5-Lucy, 6-Maggie, 7-Daisy, 8-Jake, 9-Bailey, 10-Rocky

Cats… 2-Chloe, 3-Lucy, 4-Tigger, 5-Tiger, 6-Smokey, 7-Oliver, 8-Bella, 9-Sophie, 10-Princess

Two of the most common names surprise me: Daisy and Lucy. It seems to me that a top ten list on uninsured dogs and cats might differ. One thing is certain, Gobushgooshkee would not be among them.

Not So Welcome

Might there be in existence, a species' feces identification manual? We are curious and quite perturbed. What creature has been leaving deposits on the concrete near the "Welcome" mat at the front door entrance, not a far distance from our "Leave A Note" box?

A rather large toad has been enjoying daylight hours within the drain tile buried beneath a section of concrete, also near the front entryway. Its presence was announced one evening from within an elbow that joins the drain tile to the downspout. Eerie and startling it was, that erratic, clawing, scraping sound. We thought at first perhaps a young bird had fallen into the gutter's drainage opening, but after investigation, stooped with a flashlight on the gravel into which the rainwater flows, we gazed upon a bloated figure, not at all birdlike. Surprised we were. The creature... not.

It did not seem to mind at all, our peering in. In fact, shortly after, perhaps curious as well, the critter hopped on out into the open, as if to bid us "good evening". Obviously no threat was sensed, for there it sat for quite some time, apparently comfortable, assuming "squatter's rights", enjoying the cool evening air, contemplating its next move.

At day's end, once again, much time was spent trying to coax moths and other wee beings off the screens before cranking the windows closed. It's somewhat disquieting, going to bed knowing they'll be trapped within that narrow space for the night's duration. They just don't get it. Gone as quickly as the windows open to a new day, still, in the evening, there again they are. Window opening: "We're outta here!". Window closing: Haven't got a clue. But, they do seem none the worse for having tolerated their restricted hours.

Fifty Two And Much To Do

This year's birthday was spent with the folks who brought me into this world, dear Mom and Dad, up in the U.P. Little sister shared the day as well. Three brothers between us live far-a-field. Although they were not present for such a momentous occasion, they no doubt each set aside a slice of that particular day for reflection. Yes, their tomboy sister who could outrun them all and did quite well with football, baseball, and the climbing of trees.

Sister has twelve less years upon this planet than I. Along with her generous gift came an admonition: "You cannot be 38 anymore, because that would make you younger than me." She is 39 and holding. I did blow out all of the candles, five and two, that were placed upon the beauteous cake which was accented with perfectly formed blue roses, nestled upon a dense layer of whipped cream. Beautiful flowers defying snow and frost, I mused. There were three of them; blue flowers: a symbol of personal fulfillment. Already 52 and still so much to do!

Just the night before, shortly before retiring, I had actually blurted out, "Well, this is the last day of being 41!" Sister stared at me in disbelief, and concern that I might actually be "losing it". Realizing the error stunned me. Ten years off! Staring back, eyebrows raised and as big a smile as I could muster, there was hope of convincing her… "just kidding".

Off to bed with two parental gifts in hand: "Tales Of Graceful Aging From The Planet Denial", by Nicole Hollander and, "I Feel Bad About My Neck", by Nora Ephron. Yup, the folks were surely smiling, chuckling perhaps, as they settled in for a good night's sleep. Such a blessing is humor. May we all have such blessings over the Holiday Season. And may "God bless us… everyone."

Sir Hugh Beaver

Sir Hugh Beaver, a resident of London, was enjoying a seasonal hunting expedition with companions. It was in Ireland, an autumn occasion, in the early 1950s. The group had their sights set on golden plover. Coming upon a flock of desired game birds, Beaver took aim, fired, and stood stunned in disbelief (shared by his hunting buddies), for the seasoned hunter had missed.

Later that evening, at a local pub, a discussion ensued, centered around the flight and speed of various game birds. Grouse, ducks, geese, and the plover were considered in the debate over which was the fastest game bird. A search for an answer continued outside the pub's walls. No answer was found.

After returning to London, Beaver was further dismayed, for there also no answer could be found. He considered lack of such reference information a most great deficiency for Britain. What a great idea for British pubs, he thought; a compilation of researched, authoritative answers to the questions so often raised and debated among the gentlemen who gathered for socialization, conversation and refreshment. Oh, but how to go about it?

Sir Hugh Beaver was the Managing Director of "Arthur Guinness, Son & Company, LTD". Upon mentioning his idea to the brewery's Junior Executive, a possibility arose. The latter, Chris Chataway, was an athlete, a runner. He had made the acquaintance, in his sporting life, of two young men, sons of a prominent newspaperman, who had themselves become journalists and covered sporting events. The family was one of "insatiable curiosity" said Chataway to Beaver. The brothers, Norris and Ross McWhirter, who happened to be twins, had for long been compiling their own lists of facts and trivia from various sources. Their inquiries and interests knew no bounds. Having found many discrepancies amongst their ever-growing acquisition of published "facts", they had from early on intended to establish an agency for the correction of errors. Their enterprise began in 1951 with its primary focus on the supplying of facts and figures to publications and advertisers.

Eventually the fellows did meet. The two young men were commissioned to begin work on the book. It was in the early to mid '50s, only four months after the endeavor began, that a slim volume of 198 pages was published and made available to the public. Only four months after its initial publication, the reference book became England's #1 non-fiction best-seller. It holds the record, yes it does, for the biggest selling copyrighted book ever published and is considered worldwide as an authoritative source. Such is the outline of the humble beginnings of "The Guinness Book of World Records".

The first publication included, to mention but two: Mrs. Feodor Vassilyev having given birth to 69 children in the 19th century. The Vassilyev's had 16 sets of twins, 7 sets of triplets and 4 sets of quadruplets. And the fastest land speed for a rocket sled was recorded at 632 miles per hour.

Oddly enough, forgotten in that first publication, was an answer to the question that had originally inspired the book, the question debated in the Ireland pub after a day of hunting: What is the fastest flying game bird? The omission did appear in future volumes.

As for the lack of exact dates, even years, in the relating of this information, believe it or not, from various sources did I discover, yup, factual discrepancies.

Ode To A Face

Ode to the face that gently speaks
Expressive without words
To look into such caring eyes
On darkest nights and see bright skies

To call to mind in troubled times
A so familiar glance
That pierces through all weariness
And calls the soul to dance

Ode to the face, compassionate
Embracing all around
To feel such strong, enduring love
Shining through from God above

A countenance so radiant
Though silent, still does teach
Acceptance of whatever
In this life, is out of reach

Ode to the face which through the years
Reflects life's gifts and scars
A mixture of one's joys and pain
Ever humble, never vain

From which emits a certitude
Humor, light and grace
Oh yes, I know it oh so well
It is my brother's face

"Grounded"

Twice in this life, while in a car, I've experiences the impact of another vehicle; once from behind, once from the side. The first time was tragic. The second, but noteworthy. Both times the vehicles were totaled. Neither time did I see it coming, nor was I at fault. Alcohol, rage, and a high rate of speed fueled the first. Alcohol and running late fueled the second.

A lasting result, understandably so, is a heightened sensitivity to, not only driving, but riding in a motor vehicle. Except for its affect on anxiety levels, this has been a good thing. One day last year, while approaching an intersection in which a crossroads had stop signs, the driver of a truck sailed right through. I had stopped, although I faced no stop sign, because I saw it coming.

The same holds true for last week. Southbound on Grand Ave., again with the right-of-way, a cautious approach to an intersection allowed me to see it coming: a truck barreling through (literally) the stop sign, crossed my path, but feet from my car, uprooted a power pole on the other side of the road, ploughed into the rail of the Laundromat entryway, and there it sat, pole suspended, wedged into the truck bed, behind the cab. Thank God, no one was in its path. No injuries occurred.

As wires snapped and sparks flew, before the pole rested motionless, seemingly secure, it crossed my mind that this could very well be the cue preceding entrance to another realm. Would these earthly days be over? In utter amazement, one humorous thought did cross my mind. Had a dinosaur passed by, it would've met with stunned silence. Such suspended moments are accepting of such notions.

One's immediate response is the desire to escape the situation, but the wires draped and hanging but inches from the doors' windows, as well as the first by-stander to capture my attention, reinforced rule number one: DO NOT GET OUT OF THE VEHICLE. This I knew, but may have been slow to recall. It was only when putting the car into reverse and beginning to back up that rule number two was made known to me: DO NOT MOVE THE VEHICLE (at least in this particular situation).

Others had joined the first gentleman in caringly stressing with gestures and voices: "Stay in the car! Don't move!" Messages scrawled on scraps of paper were pressed to the window: "Should I turn off the A.C.?" , "Shut off the ignition?" But firstly was a plea for someone to please phone my home. The folks were in town, as well as my brother and sister-in-law, to visit with us. I knew that Jeff was not at home. There grew an intense desire for the comforting, well-grounded (no pun intended) presence of my brother. Shortly after, he and his wife arrived to stand reassuringly with others near the scene.

For the Grace of God, past lessons learned, a brother's loving response, and the caring souls present that day… all of you, I am truly grateful and surely blessed. Always, always approach an intersection, despite not having to stop, as though those crossing your path may not. Stop signs cannot in themselves stop vehicles, only the drivers that observe them. For a vehicle without a driver, rolling downhill, a stop sign has no meaning. We must carry with us our own caution signs for the intersections of our lives.

A Point Made

Ah! At the morning window, where priceless moments occur! Those wee hummers let it be known when their feeder's nectar becomes too shallow. They flit about the window, determinedly, seeking attention for the lack, not unlike a pooch discovering its food bowl is empty, or water source depleted.

A behavior different from the acrobatic thanks, displayed after partaking of nourishment, is less showy, more intense and repetitive. Had I removed the window screen, the persistent little creature would surely have come in. After a close and most thorough surveillance through the window pane, no doubt dismayed, the tiny form actually gripped the screen and poked its beak through a miniscule screen square.

Sitting so near, I thought of the camera on the counter across the room, but remained seated in amazement for too long. After quietly rising to fetch the camera, the privilege of capturing the moment on film was denied. Expectations are so often met with disappointment. A point had been made.

It brought to mind a long-time favorite story, "The Little Prince", by Antoine de Saint Exupery. Lines from that book are engraved in my mind: "We are responsible for what we tame", and "It is only with the heart that one can see rightly; what is essential is invisible to the eye".

Our pets and other attended creatures grow to rely on us. Such a small incident, it may seem, in the large and diversified scheme of things, but in that most brief and rare moment a need outside my own, unspoken yet quite clear, touched the heart and emphasized the existence of such need far beyond the confines of a morning's view.

Again, Antoine de Saint Exupery: "A single event can awaken within us a stranger totally unknown to us. To live is to be slowly born".

Percival

A "Time Capsule" section in a recent "Wisconsin Trails" magazine focused on a James Gates Percival (1795-1856). Born in Connecticut, Percival became a Wisconsinite in 1853. Despite his genius and accomplishments, before and after arriving in our fair state, he came to be regarded as quite the eccentric, listed as one of the great ones, actually.

Percival earned a medical degree at the age of 25 from Yale University, but his practice of medicine was short-lived due to his extreme timidity. He immersed himself in a world of books. Some believe him to be the authentic author of Webster's Unabridged Dictionary, the very first one. The man is said to have known more than ten different languages! He read, journaled his observations and wrote poetry as well.

It was for the purpose of looking into matters concerning an eastern mining company's holdings that brought Percival to Wisconsin. The very next year (1854), following his settling here, Governor Barstow appointed him the state's first geologist. His days were spent within quarries and among mineral holes. Not at all a social fellow, one must wonder at his interest in learning such a variety of languages. I suppose it would be for the ability to read other than English publications.

A lone and rather unkempt chap, it seems a shame that one so knowledgeable, with so much to share, preferred written rather than verbal expression and his own silent existence to the company of others. He left this life a poor man, at least by worldly standards. Not much attention was given to his poems during his lifetime, but seven years after his death (1865, at his home in Hazel Green), one of his poetic endeavors was selected (by whom, it was not stated), set to music (again, source unknown), and sung (by whom, not a clue), prior to the "Gettysburg Address" given by President Abraham Lincoln in 1863.

Quite the legacy for one such as he. Perhaps his spirit is now embraced and partakes of heavenly waltzes, as well as the pleasure of mingling with like minds.

In Silence… Majestic

Many a soaring eagle has delighted the eyes over the years. This past year I've known the pleasure of observing them daily, sometimes perched majestically while surveying the area. Most often they're seen scanning the river below, while gliding high above the treetops. My, what amazingly sharp eyes must be required to spot their prey from such heights!

A shrill, persistent calling out of some creature drew me to the window recently. It was a sound I'd heard before, but never identified with its origin. Two eagles, one quite larger than the other, held my attention. So in sync they were in their patterns of flight; for a time one would follow closely after the other, then, side-by-side, the distance between them slowly grew. Remaining parallel to one another, they circled and swooped. Off and on, the shrill call that had drawn me to the window was repeated. I was certain that some creature was aware of the hovering birds of prey and felt threatened.

Spellbound for quite some time, I marveled at the artful grace and effortless precision of those regal birds, so in tune to each other. How did they communicate? What was it they had in sight, while so silently soaring? Silent… I thought.

It was only after closer observation (binoculars) and keener listening that I realized, it was the smaller of the two above calling out, not a creature from below. That sound was produced by that majestic bird?! Many an eagle have I seen soaring in silence. Always in silence. A voice whose source had been unknown and a creature previously with voice unknown clearly connected, while in this mind the connection struggled through static, bringing to mind the familiar, "Can you hear me now?"

No disrespect intended for that long respected symbol of our great land, but honestly, I was stunned. Imagine never having heard the voice of James Earl Jones. He appears on stage. Awaiting his address, the audience hears a voice welcoming all to the event. They look about for the speaker. No one considers it could be the man right before them, because it sounds like Truman Capote. Ah, but sure enough, the lips are moving, the gestures correspond to the utterances. Hmmm.

Johnny Cash appears on the grandstand. The "man in black" begins to sing. We hear… Barry Manilow. Yup, it was kind of like that. The enjoyment and awe of those mighty birds has in no way lessened. Rather, the wonder of them has increased. I now know the sound of an eagle. Although it is not at all as I would have imagined it, it is just as it should be.

With each new realization, it seems, limits of awareness can be stretched. The sting of failed expectations and disappointments may weaken. Tolerance and acceptance more easily expand. So much can spring from just moments in time.

Oops

The animal was not harmed during the incident leading up to this ponder. Sister arrived from Lincoln, Nebraska in a not-so-roomy vehicle which was stuffed full as a belly after Thanksgiving dinner. Returning to Wisconsin after many long years, except for occasional visits, she will be settling nearby, at least through the winter months. A pet carrier on the back seat was completely surrounded, except for the gated opening, which faced the car door, of course, allowing easy access for the occasional stretch stop during the long trip. Within the carrier was her beloved Baxter, her cat of ten years.

It was about 9:30 p.m. when she arrived at our house. Baxter would be spending the next few days at my daughter's, who also has a beloved cat, and the assortment of various feline necessities.

Sister attached collar and leash to kitty and let him out to roam about a bit. Within a few minutes he was free and heading from the well-lit driveway into the backyard darkness. It was a "snap" collar sis had attached to her precious pussycat, a collar that opens against strain so as to prevent choking. Yes, Baxter's a housecat. As sis went after Baxter, I went inside for our pup's old collar. Hansomman and Baxter are near the same size. Yup, big kitty! The collar was not where I assumed it would be. Hmmm. So, I grabbed the chain and leash hanging on a hook by the door.

Daughter was on her way. Baxter was back in the carrier. Sister was retrieving the necessary items from her car. I squatted down before the carrier, gently slipped the collar over Baxter's head and tried to coax him out with soothing words and the slightest tug. "You won't get free of this one", said I. He was not amused.

Baxter, ten years old, is quite the mellow fellow, but the next sixty seconds (at most) he behaved in the most bizarre fashion, which was amplified by the headlights beaming directly upon him as daughter pulled into the driveway. We stared in disbelief, witnessing a performance no doubt worthy of an audition and a prize. As I still held the leash in hand, sister and daughter, in unison, screamed, "What did you do?!" There was no tension on the leash, except for the few incredible airborne moments, when Baxter was observed well above eye level. Again, "What did you do?!"

Landing on all fours, as all cats do, with pent up travel energy now totally spent, Baxter glared at me. The message could not have been any clearer had the creature spoke it: "Do not approach me. You are not my friend." Sis and daughter, upon realizing the cause of the short-lived, quite dramatic scene just witnessed, were comforting "poor kitty". They too, glared at me.

Lesson learned (spoken by two, heard as from three): "You do not put a choke collar on a cat!" Baxter left, not only willingly, but eagerly, with my daughter, sensing he was now in good hands.

A Gift - In Point Of View

In a dream there stood a child in a garden, not alone
But the presence of another, although felt, was yet unknown
In silence as a new day dawned and lightened all around
A form came into focus, there at work upon the ground

Without complaint he toiled alone, a man the child knew
But never in a garden, not from this point of view
"We do not have a garden", said the child as she drew near
The man, who was her father answered, "Yes, we do my dear"

The child gazed the longest while into her father's eyes
Which more than any words expressed, did help her realize
So much of what one does in life by others is not known
Bits then of her father's life, in that dream were shown

A heart did fill with love, respect, and gratitude to be
The child of the father in the garden… the child was me
It was still dark when I awoke
A Loving Voice so gently spoke
The best of what's been given thee
Endures throughout Eternity

In Grace

In wonder we ask
Why we've been so blessed
Let us know
It is but the Grace of God
Encompassing
As we tend the garden of the spirit

How blessed to share
That which springs
From the hearts
To see ourselves
In another's eyes
To feel, in embracing
The beating of Life's eternal rhythm

On Adventure

Having read many articles and viewed numerous programs on the amazing experiences of adventurous folks, it dawned on me just how relative the term "adventurous" is. There are so many levels, such a variety for the "go for it" crowd. Having been considered by some to be a "free spirit", a "gypsy", and truly adventurous throughout many years, awhile back in time, that chapter now registers mild-to-moderate on the adventure scale.

Obtaining a three month Greyhound "Ameri-Pass" to travel about the country alone was considered adventurous by many, foolish by some, back in the mid-to-late '70s. Embarking from the Milwaukee bus station, without a plan, no schedule, no clue to what lay ahead, was exciting. "Go west" young woman, as the spirit moves you. No reservations, no stored luggage, just one backpack and a guitar in a soft-shell case accompanied me.

Up into the mountains of New Mexico (a two week stay), camping along the Colorado River in Yuma, Arizona… ah, delightful! Sleeping under the stars after searching for scorpions (yup, found a few), it had never crossed my mind back then, that they might find me.

Well, there were many wondrous, unusual and exciting experiences during that chapter of life. I spent some time in Clint Eastwood's room of his favorite San Diego hotel (nope, he wasn't there), a beautiful woman sauntered slowly past, several times, while I sat awhile amidst some local musicians in a park. Remarking on the celebrity-decked appearance, someone informed me that the person was indeed a man. Some time was spent in the home of Robert Mitchum's sister, after looking up and contacting a Bahai Faith phone number in the local Scottsdale, Arizona directory. Yup, it was she who was listed. There again, I sat a spell where a well-known actor's room was ever-ready for a visit. The resemblance to her brother was remarkable, right to the dimple in the chin. Again, nope, he wasn't there.

Just for the fun of it I sent off a letter to brother and his wife, telling them I'd met someone and joined a commune. A lengthy elaboration on a new lifestyle followed. They were not at all surprised by the contents of that letter, only by the closing: "Just kidding. Love sis".

Personal adventures came to mind after one evening's news broadcast. A woman was shown, swinging and bobbing about in mid-air, feet pointed skyward. Yet another bungee-jumper, but wait... this was a woman celebrating the approach of her 87th birthday! Nope, wouldn't do that. Nor would I trek across Alaska by dogsled, climb rocky peaks, sit upon the ocean floor within a structure no bigger than my bedroom, or mingle closely with sharks, crocs, lions and such.

There are those rare individuals that thrive on the adrenaline rush of uncommon thrills. They bounce along through the wilds in open jeeps. By sunlight, by moonlight, it matters not. Amidst the untamed beasts they meander. Out in small boats, miles and miles from land, hands reach out to touch creatures as large as busses. The wallop of a tail attached to 40 tons of motion, no matter how unintentional, is a possibility far beyond the risk most folks would cross. Adventure: relative, expansive, personally defined.

Perk Server

Disgruntled with the performance, lifespan and number of coffee makers purchased over the years, a bit of deliberating was in order. Not of the serious furrowed brow variety, just simply some serious reflection; peaceful, meditative moments, from which so often emerge elements related to a particular focus. The key to such meditative process is in maintaining the intended focus (in this case, a more efficient coffee brewing apparatus). Over the years this approach has served me well. As of late, this method has become more time consuming, which may attribute to the menopausal mind, as well as the fact that creative minds are rarely tidy. Clutter abounds.

Have you seen the commercial with Ellen Degeneres? She sits in a meditative pose. Her thoughts are on socks. Well, I found myself wondering on why folks do not immediately discard pens that no longer serve their purpose. Rather than being disposed of, they are put back into the drawer, the writing utensil holder, or simply laid down, to be picked up again. So often do we set ourselves up for disappointment.

With semi-focused mind I continued to sail upon the river of distractions. After floating along awhile with many unrelated thoughts and observations, a relevant memory eventually surfaced. As the current carried me round a bend, there we sat at a kitchen table, coffee pot between us. It was quite the heavy, old-time pot, tarnished and scarred, blackened by years of use upon flame as boiling water perked up through fragrant coffee grounds.

I always drank too much coffee when visiting that old friend. It was so good! "What's your secret to such a great pot of coffee?", I had once asked (actually during our last coffee table time together… at her home). "I never wash the pot", she replied with a shrug. So much for that meditative session.

Soon after that, however, a sleek black and silver electric percolator was selected, as well as a wee four-cup pot for those special later-in-the-day blends. It was about three weeks ago that the purchase occurred. The wee pot has been used every day. The main pot was unboxed about a week ago and sits prominently upon the counter, shiny and new, not yet prepared for its first perk.

It's actually quite lovely. Yes, decorative it is. One could envision a bouquet of garden flowers bursting forth from its tapered top, with a sprig of "Baby's Breath" and a trail of "Forget-Me-Nots" draping from the spout. Remembering the price tag deleted that picture from the mind. Quite the expensive vase that would be.

Perhaps tomorrow, or the next day, its perk-to-serve purpose will begin. For now it is enough to just enjoy its pristine presence on the counter and savor the precious moments… of prolonged anticipation.

If Only

Inherited: a mansion, furnished, every room
Famous paintings hung upon the walls
Cash and jewels within a safe, security ensured
Ornamental treasures lined the halls

Guests did come most frequently
For friends, the man had many
His fortune, oh, he wanted all to see
For little did he have before, as known by worldly measure
It wasn't long, obsessed he came to be

More important did become
Than friends he once held dear
The objects he had gained without a cost
Soon no one came to see him, so hard was it to bear
The radiant nature of a man, now lost

To worldly treasures, vain pursuits
Selfishness and greed
How better off he'd truly been before
If only he had shared such wealth
With others so in need
He could have been, he would have had, much more

Whatever

The term, "hanging out", brings to mind monkeys suspended from towering tree branches or laundry clipped to the clothesline, its drying time determined by the day's particular weather conditions. "Just chillin'", What better image for that than a male penguin rooted to one spot while embracing an egg between its feet? In the '70s we "scooped the loop". How that came to express our evening cruising through the downtown area is baffling, but doesn't make the worthy of investigation list. It brings no particular image to mind. The expression makes about as much sense as the burning up of gas to do so. It would seem not much of that goes on these days.

Such expressions must surely stump those who are struggling with English as a second language.

"Gonna hang out and chill with some friends Friday night. You in? Crank up the amps, loosen up, shoot the bull. Might swing over to Jimmy's Saturday. Always a good jam in that garage. You game?"

Have other languages grown as loose and lazy? Probably, many of them. In this fast-paced world of ours, even our thoughts get condensed and expressed in fragmented sentences, not only in abbreviated text messaging, but straight from the mouth.

When my daughter was a wee one, she once toddled into the kitchen with a request. One word: "Milk". She soon learned to add "please". Two words. Eventually a full-sentenced request was made. "Could I have some more milk, please?" Isn't it amazing that we grow up learning such things, pass through all of those required English classes of our school years, and then as adults, discover that there is a good chance many of us would not be able to pass a junior high English exam?

It was recently pointed out to me, by a gentleman who's taught grammar for many years, that I had incorrectly used the word "I" instead of "me" (or vice versa) in one of my "Ponders". He politely and patiently explained the proper usage for each. I politely and patiently listened and, by golly, it did register. Sincerely he was thanked, for as a writer it mattered to me, but it must be admitted that for a brief moment, an uttered "whatever" wisped through my mind. How odd.

"Whatever", used as a response, was not acceptable to me. My daughter can attest to that. How quick and delighted she was to react to that word issuing forth from my lips during a period of frustration. How surprised I was to have spoken it. Ah, how we do flow with the times.

One could imagine that some day "Spoken Eloquence" will become a category amidst the DVD and Audio cassette sections in our stores. For our listening pleasure (those of us who would enjoy it), we could purchase or rent recordings of tales well told. Surround Sound would enrich the experience of a journey back in time. Perhaps we might select from a variety of voices, each commanding the attention due an outstanding stage presence.

Now, it is realized that some of this is already out there, but a broader range, a higher level perhaps is yet to come. More and more may it be appreciated: The uplifting potential of eloquent speech; in its melodic delivery, so purposeful, moving… resonant.

On Hope

One without hope is empty of all expectations. Loss of hope, the state of hopelessness, brings despair. Uninvited, relentless and erosive, depression consumes. Despite the ever-growing awareness of the role brain chemistry plays in the lives of those afflicted, the embrace of relief remains unknown, unimaginable, and therefore unsought by many, oh so many, agonizing beings in this world.

According to an article which appeared in the Wall Street Journal, March of '07, "Americans are the unhappiest people on the earth." A study, done by both the World Health Organization, along with the Harvard Medical School, revealed that of fourteen nations surveyed, America ranked highest in population percentage for those suffering from both depression and bi-polar disorder... 9.6%. In comparison: Lebanon-6%, Mexico-4.8%, Italy-3.8%, Japan-3.1%, Nigeria-0.8%. It is believed that in the more impoverished societies, greater focus is placed on family, religion, and cultural traditions, which provide "comfort and meaning".

Yes, this is a sorrowful chord to strike, what with the upcoming Holiday Season and all that it entails. All that it entails... Let us pause with that for a few moments and see what comes to mind, - past the shopping and the santas, beyond the glitter and the gifts. Shorn of all its ornaments, outward symbols and signs, at the very core of all festivities, a Message resounds. Clear in its delivery, profound in its significance: "Love one another." A most precious gift - in reaching out to one in need. Each and every one of us, for someone else, can make a difference.

For those who have not dwelt within that state of despair, it is impossible to imagine. For those within that realm of hopelessness, one caring heart may influence. A deeper understanding of, and various treatments for mental illnesses are broadening. Yet, far too many remain unaware. In their seeming aloneness they struggle. Their worlds become, oh so small and dark, no doors or windows. So it seems.

But, always will there be doors of hope, windows of light. May they find them. If not, may they be opened to them by others. To those who suffer such an affliction, seek out help. That first step is the key to realizations, the first of which is that you are not alone. There is value, there is purpose for every human being.

In the words of a most caring, loving soul, Shoghi Effendi :

"The troubles of this world pass, and what we have left is what we have made of our souls; so it is to this we must look - to becoming more spiritual, drawing nearer to God, no matter what our human minds and bodies go through."

Let us love one another.

Gifts Of Heaven

The winds of Heaven blow
Free of rain, sleet and snow
Wafting fragrant
Soft, caressing breezes
Reach us here

The streams of Heaven flow
Living waters, crystal glow
Pearl-laden waterfalls
Showering upon us pearls of wisdom
Patiently they lie within their shells

The melodies of Heaven sound
Heard faintly by those earthly bound
Muffled by all worldly noise
Lingering where silence
Has been fled

The gifts of Heaven do abound
But willfully we stand our ground
Intentions, without Guidance
Swept away by surging tides
Leaving us, as often does the weather
Stunned and unprepared

Heaven's breezes, Heaven's streams
Melodies and gifts of dreams
Ever-present, never ceasing
Reaching out to trusting souls
In open hearts
Rejoicing in surrender

An Admiration

A large, majestic red-tailed hawk perched motionless for quite some time high up within a tree along the river. Whether scanning for prey, pausing to rest, digest, or simply to contemplate its next move, who knows? But, one wonders nonetheless.

Whatever the reason, he/she remained absolutely still as seven or eight raucous and hefty crows apparently had nothing better to do than disturb the peace. Looking for a bit of excitement on an otherwise uneventful day? Carrying a grudge? Felt they had dibs on that particular tree? No way of knowing, but again, one wonders.

Anyway, the noisy, determined group succeeded in flushing the much larger bird from its perch. I thought of rear-view mirrors, as those less bold, threw peer pressure to the wind and quickly left the vicinity. "Objects are larger than they appear."

Surprised they were, it seemed, by the hawk's magnificent wingspan. I surely was. It would require more than a few Danny DeVitos to pose a threat to Arnold Schwartzenneger. Even so, the more determined continued their harassment and pursuit; swooping, diving, trailing... playing "chicken" in the sky. One by one the crows withdrew, flapping off to who knows where. Yup, best to retreat before energy depletion.

The hawk continued to soar about, now undisturbed. I resolved to work towards facing life's unexpected occurrences and difficulties with the soaring acquiescence of a mighty hawk among raucous crows. Might that be possible? 'Tis a worthy goal.

A New Pup

We have a new puppy, runt of the litter, passed over by those who selected her litter-mates. Unable to fend for herself, she was mothered and bottle-fed by the breeder. A dear friend informed me of the wee one's situation: six-months-old and still unspoken for. The other pups had each been purchased for a considerable sum. This frail, loveable, feather-weight was given to us because she needed a loving home, and thanks to my friend, the breeder was assured she would have one.

Yup, love at first sight. She seemed to like us as well. I nearly held my breath as my guys, Jeff and the Hansomman (peek-a-poo), looked her over and got acquainted. Jeff seemed quite amused as the tidbit canine boinged up and down on her back feet (to waist high!) and then pranced about like she was in charge of the establishment.

Hansomman was not impressed: quite disinterested actually. That was a good thing... two "yeahs" and one "whatever". Home with us she came. Two days passed. The precious addition to the family familiarized herself with the new surroundings, settling in contentedly.

Day three... still no name. Perhaps we tried too hard. Many came to mind, but all were dismissed. Finally, while occupied with other concerns, out of the blue came to me, "Hansel and Gretel". Hmmm. Go figure. Anyway, peek-a-poo and yorkie-poo are now our Hansom and Gretta.

But Why?

A book has been written, around for quite some time now, about why bad things happen to good people. It wouldn't be hard to locate one, for the subject is the title of the book. I've not read it, but intend to. It is on one of my lists, somewhere.

Having pondered that for many a year (no, not consistently nor obsessively), I've achieved a level of acceptance on the matter… more than a few times, for when things are going well it's easy to forget and one must tackle it anew. Like learning a foreign language, when not exposed to its usage, clarity fades. I wish to read what a published author has to say on that subject, so as to compare our views.

Many folks who take to writing aspire to eventually publishing a novel. I've started three, at various points in time. They've been neglected long enough, for inspiration wanes, that they have become interwoven in my mind. They shall now have to be disentangled from one another, or combined. This will be a priority this year, along with the compiling of thoughtful, meditative notes on why bad things happen to people who are doing good things. No, the subject will not be the title of that book.

So often, while engaged in doing a favor for another, or various other good deeds, one meets with misfortune. I've touched on this subject before, having achieved a level of acceptance and meditative insights… again, more than a few times.

Recently, a good portion of the morning was spent tending to multiple tasks for another who has been delayed in returning from a trip out-of-state. After completing the tasks, enter: MISFORTUNE. Briefly, it involved the impact of my S10 pick-up's right side rear section with the back corner of a trailer. TOTALLY MY FAULT. Damage to the trailer was minimal. Actually, not the trailer itself, but only a fraction of a reflector chipped off. The individual was most kind and would not accept my insistent offer to replace it.

Assuming that the truck's bumper had but nicked the trailer, the young man's reaction, and the fact that no greater harm had been done filled me with relief… until, following his gaze and hearing the words, "Look at your truck." The bumper had played no part in the unfortunate occurrence. The tail pipe appeared to have extended itself. The panel directly above it was caved in and scarred with a long, deep gash, the result of having intruded upon the trailer's metal-covered corner. Once again, the all too familiar internal scream, "WHY DO BAD THINGS HAPPEN TO PEOPLE WHO ARE DOING GOOD THINGS?"

Beyond the obvious, human error, that question continued to gnaw at me. It hovered over the more urgent considerations of insurance/deductible. Once again I retraced old thought patterns that had been processed so many times that it is a wonder they have not led to conditioned responses of a more accepting nature.

The answer to that question has eventually and always been received as a question itself: "Will you continue to do good things despite the fact that bad things happen?" I can honestly and gratefully answer, "Yes." But, so far, the process involved after such occurrences has repeated itself. Perhaps next time, for surely there will be one, I will remember… and forego the self-torment.

Neurobic Brain Gym

According to one of the books I'm reading (another gem from mom), multi-tasking would be considered good for the aging brain. It has been amazingly determined, through scientific method, that "new brain cells are generated in adult humans." Keeping it simple: we do use it or lose it. There are branches on nerve cells (dendrites) that deal with information via connections (synopses). Unused, unchallenged, the dendrites thin out. Not only can we grow and thicken dendrites in our aging brains... we can "grow, adapt, and change patterns of connections."

Enter: Neurobics - for overall mental fitness. Unlike other brain exercises, such as logic puzzles, Neurobic exercises use combinations of the senses (sight, smell, touch, taste, and hearing), as well as emotions. New connections and patterns between different areas of the brain are created and strengthened. Brain nutrients (neurotrophins) are produced.

According to the Neurobics approach, mental activity = self-help. "Everyday life is the Neurobic Brain Gym." Experiencing the unexpected and the intentional use of all the senses throughout the day enhances our mental agility. It is suggested that small changes in routines and habits can be "mind building", and increase mental flexibility. Our brains thrive on engaging new tasks, being challenged, and yes, even frustrated.

Three conditions are key to employing the Neurobic approach to our daily lives:

1) Involve one or more of the "senses" in a novel context. Rely on senses not normally used for a specific task. Example: Get dressed for the day with your eyes closed.

2) Engage attention. Stimulation kicks in an alert mode. Example: Turn the pictures on your desk upside down.

3) Break with routine in a significant way. Example: Take a new route to work.

The Neurobic approach to strengthening the human brain involves all of the senses, embraces the unexpected, and challenges us to break with routine. Simple. Painless. Affordable. The book is only $8.95!! It can even be amusing. Brushing your teeth with the left hand, if right-handed, is in some way like stretching a muscle in the mind. The adult brain can be nourished. It can "rewire", as well as grow new "wires". The brain's neurotrophin production is dependent on activity which forms "neural branches and connections." The process is compared to a self-fertilizing garden. How cool. How exciting. How wondrous is that?!

The book: "Keeping Your Brain Alive: 83 neurobic exercises to help prevent memory loss and increase mental fitness", by Lawrence C. Katz, PHD and Manning Rubin

Chosen Issues

If the human species was nearing extinction, a shift in perspective would no doubt occur. Health care, education, homelessness… and a myriad other issues, now endlessly debated, would perhaps, in a more self-less and truly consultative manner, be resolved. Must an unprecedented sense of urgency spread throughout our world, an engulfing convulsion shake us to the core?

Shocks are administered to sufferers of depression for whom all other treatments have failed. Considered drastic measures by some, and not without its side-effects, the ends justify the means for many.

One purpose of being involved in a "cause" is surely to do some good on a manageable level amidst the chaos of the world's traumas, so overwhelming. Concern for endangered species, the eco-system, balance; these things are understandable. But, the re-introducing of a species to an area unfrequented for ages seems a bit over the top. This train of thought sprung from hearing of jaguar sightings in our country's southwest. Four had been sighted, last I heard, in both Arizona and New Mexico. Crossing the border from Mexico, they are considered neither "illegal" nor "alien". In fact, not only is much attention being given to their presence, their movements, and protection, but the possibility exists that they could re-establish themselves in the area.

This has become, for some, a dilemma: How can we keep out the "illegal aliens", yet maintain an inviting passage for the jaguar? This is seen, again by some, as desirable. Wild, free-roaming jaguars, in a major tourist-outing-vacation-retirement area… hmmm. I recall watching, while camping along the Colorado River in Yuma, Arizona, as people quietly made their way north across that river, during the night. Jaguars… not a one. Fine by me.

Intangible

The marvel of heart-felt connections come often to mind; those beyond the ties of family and shared histories. What so draws us to another (not talking romantic chemistry/infatuation) and causes us to look forward to their presence, delight in their company? It is not tangible. It is not a physical phenomenon, though it can express through laughter, eye contact, mannerisms, voice. There are those with whom we could sit quite a spell, just a'smiling, content, basking in the mingling of auras, sensing a palpable weaving of threads… kindred spirits waltzing to ethereal melody.

How could the spirit's essence ever be denied, when its presence is expressed as continuously as breathing? Ah! Unless one is experiencing difficulty with breath, or focused on it in some activity (yoga, etc.), we really don't pay it no mind.

In a society in which so much focus is given to reaching out, grasping, and endeavoring to possess those things which give us pleasure, or at least the illusion of… we forget, as stated so well in "The Little Prince", a book which has long been a favorite of mine: "What is essential is invisible to the eye."

Getting On With It

Isn't it amazing how both wild and domesticated creatures intuitively know the value of warming up"? Aroused from slumber, an animal will stretch, bend, reach and squat. Patiently, in the moment, muscles are extended. Joints are eased into use. Short of being in some way threatened, or missing out on a meal... or morsels, the routine continues until they're good and ready to get on with, well, whatever.

We humans, oftentimes, need herd up together in order to perform, and therefore benefit from, such activity. We even pay to do so. A group setting makes all the difference. How odd that we can prepare and transport ourselves to locations away from home to accomplish something that we struggle against doing ourselves, at home, any time of the day.

It seems a couple of weeks have passed since deciding to get back to a good routine... tomorrow. We can become quite irritable when putting off, or neglecting, those things we've intended to do. This became quite obvious one morning while out in the backyard with Gretta (puppy). Pre-dawn it was. The ground was mucky, the air sleety, and the wind was biting. There I stood, waiting for her to do her "business", and growing impatient with her prolonged preparations to get moving.

"Good grief, Gretta! Come one, get on with it. You're only nine-months-old. How stiff could you be? How many kinks could you possibly have?" No answer. She then went on to spend an equal amount of time in search of a suitable spot to do what had to be done. How exactly is that determined? I wonder. She circled many an area, not to her satisfaction, before returning to the initial site. How odd, but it seems to be the critter's way. No such behavior had ever accompanied earlier indoor mishaps. Then the behavior would have been most welcomed, a warning as to what was about to occur.

Anyway, after the initial irritation subsided, I realized again what a gift she truly is. Happy and ready to get on with the day, she had just demonstrated so clearly and simply: You do what you gotta do,
however you gotta do it.

Unexpected Inspiration

Inspiration often comes to us in such unexpected ways. After placing an ad this past year to sell a once cherished Martin guitar, it was brought to my attention, by my daughter who had looked it up online, that its value far exceeded what I may have sold it for.

A gentleman, interested in the fine instrument, called to inquire before the ad could be cancelled. We had a wonderful and lengthy conversation. He was still interested in acquiring it, even at the significantly greater price, but instead, he shared with me his love of music and input on the quality and ever-increasing value of the particular guitar I own. He not only convinced me to get reacquainted with it, but invited me to join him and his friends for an evening of playing. I did, and continue to do so, most every Wednesday evening.

Inspired by a gentleman's phone call and initial meeting, I now have four new friends, each one unique, inspiring and a light to this heart. The guys: Steve (the caller), Dennis (hub of the group, although he doesn't see himself as such), Dave (always missed when his busy schedule keeps him away), and Ed (who brought me back to the banjo by bringing his to me).

Four guys and a gal, enjoying a second wind. What once I'd not even imagine, is now yet another joyous blessing in this life.

What On Earth?

The buzzing was borderline nightmarish, growing louder, more frantic and intense. From what direction was it coming? How soon would they arrive? Where could I hide? Wait a minute… There were no wasps or bees in that movie - the one with dinosaurs brought back from the past by crazy men messing with the natural scheme of things. If there were, the stingers of such creatures could well be the size of… what?

It's only a movie. It's only a movie. No, not even a movie. You are dreaming. Eyes now open, arising from a nap, I peered through each window, searching out the source. I considered this a courageous action. Nothing to be seen. Then came silence. Hmmm.

A wasp smacked up against the window screen. I amused myself by imagining it was laughing at me. It appeared far less threatening, in comparison to the Jurassic images. I laughed back. Not much time passed and the buzzing resumed, followed by what could easily have been a crack of thunder. From the usual perch at the corner window, I witnessed the felling of a tree. No one yelled, "timber!". The tree, on a property a couple of lots from us, seemed to pause in its descent toward the river, bringing to mind one parting company, waving one last good-bye.

The source had been hidden by trees: a chainsaw, an ordinary chainsaw, operated by a competent tree-felling guy. I sat awhile, envisioning a pterodactyl circling overhead, a raptor patiently biding its time, eyes intent upon a potential morsel, and a T-Rex, just basking in the sun. As thrilling, as exciting, as that actually occurring might be, for maybe a matter of moments, I much prefer the eagles, cranes and other present day creatures. Yup, even the bees and wasp guys.

Nature's Caress

Early morning sunbeams bedazzle the nearby river
Fragmented into diamonds, they dance upon the water
Orchestrated, in place, by a current that has no other hold on them
Daylight's version of star-studded nights

Cloud shadows glide across sprawling fields
Bestowing caresses, uniting earth to sky
In the swiftness of their passing is reflected
Their dependence on the sun
Sun and shadow, contrast, ever-changing

The sky darkens
Gentle breezes; peaceful, soothing, softly humming
Silenced. All is still. Calm before the storm
Scattered notes; discordant, erratic
Rush to find their place in the approaching symphony

On Blessings

We count our blessings. Most often the counting includes such as our health, family, friends. We're thankful for our safety, security, means of livelihood. Sometimes, in remembering those less fortunate, we include such as sight, hearing, speech and mobility. We're thankful for our freedom, our choices, and ability to express ourselves.

Less frequently, perhaps rarely, do we consider as blessings any circumstances or experiences that run counter to our will; such things as simply not having our way, only to realize later, it was for the best.

Or, being at wit's end, we may come to discover that, by golly, sure enough, there's another inch or two for hanging on to, and… it's enough. Painful experiences which we cannot imagine ever getting through, are one day looked back upon. We survived.

The compassion for others which expands as a result of our own losses, the capacity for empathy which grows as a result of our own sufferings, are blessings that unite us, blessings that endure. We challenge our bodies through effort and exercise. Our bodies are challenged by misfortunes and trauma. We challenge our minds through inquiring, learning, imagining. Our minds are challenged by stresses and dilemmas.

Integrity, fortitude… loving kindness, mercy, forgiveness… Countless are the blessings of spirit, in the attainment of virtues; the very ones we reach out for in prayer, to an All-Bountiful Creator Who has given us life. Blessings everlasting.

On Confidence

A friend shared with me a comment he had recently heard, concerning "lack of confidence". Most, if not all of us, have experienced that. For some, a lack of confidence is extreme. Dreams are not realized. Risks are not taken. Potential is thwarted. Classes, programs, self-help books and therapy address the issue of self-esteem.

A healthy acceptance, respect, and belief in one's self enriches one's life. Confidence enables us to open new doors, to express our opinions, to attempt the untried despite the possibility of failing. With healthy self-esteem one realizes that a failed attempt does not make one a "failure".

Back to the comment, the gist of which was, a bit on the other hand. In moments when confidence is lacking, we are humbled. Humility, itself, opens doors. Seen in a positive light, lack of confidence poses a challenge, a stirring up of possibilities, and opportunity to delve deep within ourselves… to discover and tend to the seeds of our potentials.

Lack of confidence, in light of its accompanying humility, loses its negativity. In humility we are more likely to turn to that "Power greater than ourselves". In our humility, we may experience a greater awareness of the unfathomable vastness of which we are all a part. We gather strength. We gather courage. We build up confidence. We trust in God.

Space Garbage

What's frozen solid, exists in various sized fragments, and poses a threat as it hurls along at rates from 14,000 to 38,000 miles per hour? One might hope this to be a silly riddle, but no, the answer is an astronomical fact. Here's a hint: Last year NASA repositioned a satellite more than half a mile from its previous location. Why?

Hold on to your rockets folks! The satellite (Terra) was moved out of the path of an approaching chunk of junk, 15 inches wide, just one of nearly 12,000 (so far identified) pieces of space trash measuring more than four inches across. There are hundreds of thousands measuring between one-half and four inches, and fragments less than one-half inch number in the millions. The majority of documented trash in space exists within 1,200 miles of our planet, most of it in orbital paths, 500, 620, and 930 miles away. 38,000 mph = 11 miles per second, which is about 19 times the velocity of a bullet. In a vacuum, at three miles per second, a nylon pellet can pass through an aluminum plate. At higher speeds it can blast a significant dent into a solid lead block. Collisions are energy-violent.

Damage to the windshield of the Challenger space shuttle is believed to have been caused by a minute paint chip. After impact, it left a scar one-tenth of an inch deep. The solar panels of the Hubble Telescope were replaced in 2002. NASA determined impact sites to number 725,000. Nothing was destroyed, just rendered less effective. Rocket fragments and fuel tanks are among the discarded equipment. There's plenty of trash out there, the amount ever-increasing because of collisions which create more pieces.

The article from which this information was obtained (March/April issue of Science Illustrated Magazine -08) actually stated that "collisions are rare". According to my calculations, backed up by the old trusty calculator, 725,000 impacts over an eight year period would amount to 90,625 impacts per year. I would suppose that when dealing with the vastness of space and the concept of infinity, those figures could qualify as rare, relatively speaking. It is hard to imagine it being considered so by any folks outside of the space-science line of work.

It is said that there are 3,100 satellites orbiting Earth. Only 40% of those are functional. The rest... just hanging. Three proposed solutions are being looked into. One: Tracking the junk to prevent collisions. This is on-going. Two: Satellite shields to better protect what we put up there. Three: Retire old equipment properly. This would require getting it down into the atmosphere where it would most likely blaze out during its earth-bound journey or sending it further out, into "graveyard orbit", away from our working satellites.

So, if there is intelligent life out there, which no doubt there must be… Let us introduce ourselves. Here's some stuff we no longer need.

A Luminous Example

Every now and then we become aware of another's life story and experience a tremendous shift in our own perceptions. As we marvel at the acceptance and fortitude demonstrated by others, facing the challenges in their lives, we are touched, humbled, and inspired. Some stories are extremely profound in magnifying the blessings abounding beneath outward appearances, which may drape us in despair.

One such story is of a couple whose firstborn child entered this world, not only without eyes, but unable to walk. At first it was most difficult to bear. They cried out to God, "Why?" Not much time passed before the couple chose to focus on ability, rather than disability, on gratitude rather than despair.

Music was an important element in their lives. They shared this with their child. By the age of two the youngster could play out simple tunes on the piano. As he grew, though confined to a wheelchair, he played trumpet in the school band. His father learned the band formations and as a team they performed with others on the field.

At the age of nineteen, this young man is now a college student, talented musician, singer and composer, intent on an ever greater degree of independence. Most importantly though, he is a luminous example… of acceptance, of faith, of inner strength and inner sight. The parents, who early on nurtured and challenged that child, opened doors for him to become all that he could be. Two younger brothers, not "handicapped", have learned much from him.

John Henry Hughes truly believes he is blessed in his blindness to outward appearances, for he is more in tune with what lies within, not only within himself, but others as well.

Faded Dreams

Dreams do fade. They get set aside like books worth saving, on a shelf, out of view. They gather dust as years go by, as we deal with the demands of our changing, or changeless priorities. We forget them. Or, perhaps, we simply ignore them, for they've been trivialized or ridiculed by others, to whom we've given the power to judge what we believe to be significant.

Obstacles, antagonism, lack of confidence, the inability to redefine ourselves when the familiar crashes down around us; for so many reasons, our dreams do fade. Like those visions during sleep, we later try to recall, because we know there was something within them worthy of contemplation. Yet, we found no time to reflect when the images were fresh and clear. We made no time to even stretch, to breathe, to refresh ourselves, to gather up our energies to greet a new day with a different perspective.

Dreams do fade. Dormant they lie within us, left to dwell among suppressed child-like wonders, curiosities, the sense of adventure, of risk. We waver when faced with life's vast unknowns. Yet, they may be brought back into focus, as surely as a dwindling fire responds to kindling, and effort. Embers remain. Always. They need but be remembered, tended, believed in, realized.

Ode To Those Long Wedded

Ode to lasting marriages
To couples who've always been true
For better or worse, through sickness and health
For honoring those words, "I do"
In this world today, it's wondrous to meet
Couples who've shared many years
Whose children have grown and bring grandchildren home
Who share laughter and joy, struggles and tears

Ode to those partners who've managed
To weather, without and within
The tempests of life and its trials,
Who know when to stand firm and when to give in
Couples who have been married
For longer than I've been on earth
Sincerely I offer respect and applause
For whatever that may be worth

Ode to those soulful unions
With circles of influence wide
Enduring and sound, much flows out to all
From two who remain side-by-side

Gold Facts

A page, entitled "20 Things You Didn't Know About Gold", appeared in the December '07 Special Issue of Discover Magazine. Here are a few interesting items:

- The Aztec word for gold is teocuitlatl, which means "excrement of the gods".

-The first documented discovery of gold in the U.S. was in North Carolina, 1799. A fellow by the name of Conrad Reed found a 17-pound rock on the family farm. For three years it was used as a doorstop. Soon after, it was identified by a jeweler who managed to purchase it from Reed's father for a mere $3.50 (not even one-thousandth of its actual value). Today a seventeen-pounder would bring in over $100,000. That lump in the field eventually led to the establishment of the country's first commercial gold mine.

- A one-ounce gold piece can be transformed into fifty miles of wire, five micrometers thick (one-tenth the diameter of a human hair) or a translucent sheet five-millionths of an inch thick!

- Over 20% of the world's decorative gold is threaded into Indian saris.

- The U.S. ranks highest in the world's gold reserves.

- The earth's largest reservoirs of gold are the oceans, which are estimated at about 10 billion tons. There it shall remain until a practical way to get at it is devised.

- A single asteroid, Eros, contains more gold than has ever been mined on our planet.

- For over 20 years, regular injections of gold (in liquid suspension) was standard treatment for rheumatoid arthritis. It acted as an anti-inflammatory. Doctors are still puzzled as to why.

- The gold age actually overlaps with the Stone Age. Decorative gold objects have been found in Bulgaria which date back to 4,000 B.C.

- Gold is virtually indestructible and highly recyclable. Approximately 85% of all gold ever found is still somewhere out there today. So they say.

A Tidbit

With April swiftly approaching, here's an interesting tidbit plucked form a book: "Calendars Of The World - A Look At Calendars & The Ways We Celebrate", by Margo Westrheim.

April Fool's Day is connected with the Julian and Gregorian calendars of Christendom. The practice of "fooling" family, friends and neighbors on this particular day, April 1st, centered around the fact that April 1st, before 1564, was widely observed as the beginning of a new year. It was a time for celebration and the exchanging of gifts.

More than 400 years ago, in France, a reformed calendar was adopted. Under the rule of King Charles 1X (1564), the new year was to begin on January 1st. Regardless, many continued on with the old and familiar, refusing to acknowledge the change. In doing so, they became targets for tricks and jokes, played on them by others who deemed them "April Fools" for still observing April 1st as New Year's Day.

Although there exist three main divisions of Christian Faith: Roman Catholic, Eastern Orthodox, and Protestant, customs vary widely among them, as well as within further divisions now numbering several hundred differing sects. There are many interesting details concerning the history of evolving calendars; in the two mentioned, as well as numerous others.

The pursuing of pranks on April Fool's Day seems harmless enough, but reflecting on its origins has changed my view of it and I cannot help but wonder at how many other observations and practices continue without question, without understanding… not even curiosity. Hmmm. Go figure.

To Begin

Seems the list is long, of things we think we cannot do
Time passes and so much goes unfulfilled
We wonder, oh why bother, it's too late, oh dare I try?
Dreams hover out of reach because they're stilled

So like childhood wonderments, grown muffled over time
Forgotten or just simply laid aside
We hesitate at chances, opportunities to grow
And safely in our comfort zones abide

We may choose to coast along, afraid to stretch the life we know
To encompass more, to share what lies within
But, to nurture latent, hidden gems, is to more fully live
What better time than now to begin?

Mid-Life

Middle-age brings to mind harvest pumpkins: ripe, firm and solid on the vine… they were. No one is exactly like another. Like us, they have their similarities and differences. Some are short and squat. Some are tall and rather slender. Some have one or more unexpected bulges here and there. Most have a flat spot and at least a few scars. Mature. A bit weathered. At their peak. A "perfect" one is hard to find. But, no matter how outwardly perfect any of them appear to be, it is but for a time. All will succumb to decline.

The Autumn-time for mature pumpkins varies according to what they are chosen for. For this "Ponder" to continue, we shall enter the "Display" department, where beauty is truly in the eye of the beholder and those associated with any particular one, hang in there with it 'til the end. Some will be prominently displayed, just as they are, distinguished in size (humongous to tiny), shape (perhaps an hour-glass figure), or outstanding irregularities (looks kind of like a scrunched up little teapot, no?).

Some will be adorned, painted, given faces and hair. Others will be carved. We are drawn to them, their endless variety of faces, illumined in darkness by candles placed within; candles which need be protected from the ever-changing elements of the world around them, lest their light be extinguished. Time passes. Their structures weaken. Distinct lines soften. The light source is removed and they return to be absorbed by the earth from which they grew.

Unlike the harvest pumpkins, our Autumn days serve a far greater and expansive purpose. We continue to grow, to learn, to stretch beyond the restricted frame of existence. Tended, our flames may grow ever-brighter and our inner lights will continue to shine, throughout the winter of our lives… into an Eternal Spring.

Stilt Walker

A young man recently completed a trek, which began on May 5th, in Lambertville, MI (lower MI), near the Ohio border, to Ironwood, MI, in the upper peninsula. It was a journey of 830 miles. Neil Sauter, of Blissville, MI, was intent on raising funds for United Cerebral Palsy (UCP). He, himself, has the disease; a mild case affecting only his legs. Along the chosen route he spoke to community groups, at schools and camps. Folks were most kind. He was offered meals, bottled water, overnight accommodations, as well as donations. Some gave him a break from his backpack by carrying it alongside him to the next stop.

Sauter averaged about 20 miles per day. The excursion was made all the more remarkable because… it was done on stilts, aluminum drywall stilts, covered by custom-made trousers. Quite the wide stride. He was boosted up in height to 8'8" tall! Having learned to walk on stilts for participation in festivals and parades just the past summer, he went on to complete, on those stilts, last October's Grand Rapids' Marathon.

For Sauter's walk across MI, a three-to-one matching grant was secured by the UCP in the state, from the U.S. Dept. of Education. An estimated $15,000 fund-raising goal then soared to $60,000. Those many dollars, after expenses, will all go toward supporting UCP'S Assistive Technology Loan Fund, which offers aid for people with disabilities. Assistance with communications, mobility, and home modifications are provided.

Sauter has a bachelor's degree in psychology and has worked as a faculty member at a community college. He has also worked at a day center for those with disabilities. He intends to marry this Fall, as well as pursue a master's degree in Natural Resource Management at Michigan State University. This story came to me via the "Ironwood Daily Globe", a U.P. newspaper. Those interested in more info: website: stiltstory.org

Scientist Of The Year

A special issue of "Discover" magazine (Dec. '07) featured "Scientist of the Year - David Charbonneau". The 33-year-old Harvard University Astronomer is searching for evidence of life among the more than 200 planets now known to orbit their nearby stars. New ones are discovered each year. They are referred to as exoplanets.

Charbonneau, with his team in 1999, was the first to observe such a planet, one whose path includes a stretch between its parent star and Earth. A technique known as the "transit method" is employed to acquire data.

My comprehension of that does not even enter the category of minimal. Honestly, it's pretty much nonexistent. However, I do marvel at, and have much respect for the open, probing, scientific mind. I've no doubt that there are other worlds, other realms, life unknown to us within the vastness of God's creations. Much that was once unimaginable is commonplace today.

Surely there are countless other discoveries to be made, veiled wonders yet to be observed, hidden mysteries awaiting revelation. There always have been. It would seem that there always will be. I wonder who first said, "You ain't seen nothing yet."

Although much of the article dissipated, rather than register in this brain, the gist of it stuck with me. There are planet hunters, pioneers compelled to question, investigate, reach beyond and reconsider known boundaries. Two particular sentences from that article were especially significant to this ponderer, who is now compelled to pass them on. They are simple, yet profound. They are brief, yet potentially stimulating to all minds.

David Charbonneau:

1) "It's only with accepting a level of risk that there's the possibility of a truly novel discovery."

2) "No one was looking because we had entrenched ideas."

Entrenched ideas, unquestioned beliefs, and blind acceptance of the comfortable and familiar have, throughout our history on this planet, prolonged many a "novel discovery", as well as many an obvious one, no doubt.

Just How It Is

"Hark!", the heralding geese did sing, their greeting to a new year's Spring

A robin was spotted the day before, by a friend who eagerly watched for more

Turkeys returned a couple weeks ago, to feed at the edge of the river, so...

The Winter's snow will soon be gone. Folks gear up to tend the lawn

Spring fever now among us spreads. More easily rise the sleepy heads

Envigored, embracing the familiar, yet new. Morning frosts soon to be morning dew

Hours in the sun, oh the smell of fresh soil. Trees, plants and flowers - to them was I loyal

But challenges come in this life to us all. As for me, things have changed. I now yearn for the Fall

Winter was welcomed, outside could I tarry. For gone were the creatures of which I've grown wary

Threatened by hornets, by wasps and by bees, for the last time stung brought me down to my knees

Angry, resentful, "Woe is me!", did I cry, last summer as I felt life was passing me by

Many times stung o'er the years, I did muse, but now I'm allergic... most unwelcome news

An Epi-pen with me, wherever I go, acceptance of change often comes rather slow

Toward Zero Tolerance

On a morning news broadcast, as other news was being spoken, there appeared within the simultaneous scroll at screen's bottom, the unspoken announcement that someone had been sentenced to four and a half years in prison after driving while intoxicated. It was the individual's ninth offense. Nine times?!

There is a country, one of the Scandinavian ones, I believe, that has zero tolerance for first time offenders. One time, driving drunk, results not only in a revocation of one's driving privileges, but in ownership of a vehicle as well. The driving days are over.

It seems that we are at the opposite end of the tolerance spectrum. Hmmm. Why is that? If penalties were more severe, the very first time, would there not be a more significant impact on the issue? Many have become far too comfortable and casual within moving vehicles that carry the potential of doing horrendous damage, even at low rates of speed. Folks sail along highways while eating, drinking, smoking, talking on the phone, disciplining their children and playing music loud enough to cause vibration. Vehicles are driven by those who are overly tired, angry, rushed, medicated and pre-occupied.

It is inconceivable to me that anyone could get behind the wheel while in an impaired state. Those who do so would probably exert much effort to prevent their own loved ones and others from doing so. Many of us have heard such statements as, "I got so wasted last night, it's a wonder I ever made it home." "I can handle it… never been pulled over yet." Such statements are often delivered laughingly, arrogantly, boastfully, uncaringly. It sickens me to be aware of such an epidemic in our society; to hear on a regular basis of repeat offenders. Once is deserving of severe repercussions. Twice is unacceptable. How could anyone ever, ever commit such an offense for the ninth time?!

Endurance

In the midst of a meadow a mighty tree stood
Ancient it was, all were sure
That if it could speak, no doubt it would
Of all that's required to endure

Patience is vital, acceptance a must
Adherence to principles, noble and just
Love is essential, compassion sincere
Gratitude, hope, and ears willing to hear

Courage to face whatever lies ahead
Encompassing vision, a spirit well-fed
Letting go of the past, faith rooted and true
Gives birth to a certitude no storm can undo

Forgiveness of self, as well as of others
Acknowledging that we're all sisters and brothers
The power of prayer through God's Grace Divine
Awareness that grows to embrace all mankind

Heart-warming

It was a sorrowful sight, watching him. With an expression of stunned disbelief, canine companion at his side, he stopped to pick up the motionless bird, "What did you do? Bad! Bad dog!"

Such a variety of birds each day at the feeders, in the trees, flitting about, enjoying the yard. Each birdhouse seems to be occupied, mostly swallows. Fine by us. Quite bold and acrobatic they are. A pair of bluebirds had succeeded in securing and establishing their abode in one birdhouse facing, and nearest to, the window best suited for observation of our feathered friends.

Hansomman has often chased wee creatures about the yard, more for the enjoyment of pursuit than with the intent to catch. He has long been as good a mouser as most cats. He's chased squirrels up trees, chipmunks under rocks, deer out of the yard, making clear he'd prefer they remain on the other side of the river. He has often stirred up birds and sent them flying. Playful. Enjoyable. Declaring his turf.

A male bluebird that day was attacked. Unaware, probably pulling a worm from the soil for its young. We'd noticed that both birds fed the tiny, ravenous creatures who called out incessantly until they'd had there fill.

It was a sight to warm the heart, watching him tend to the tiny bluebirds. He'd determined the female was surely weary, trying to manage on her own. Turning the soil, gathering worms, then standing patiently and still, he fed a countless number of squiggly food into their gaping mouths, making sure each had their fill. When finished, he turned up a few more from the ground and laid them atop the mounting pole, directly above the nest, so the mama bird had easy access.

At first she seemed a bit distraught, flitting about to various perches, keeping an eye on the man so near her young. But, not for long. By the end of the day she had accepted him. She rested nearby as he continued each day to assist her. When he'd finished, she would fetch the worms from above, one by one. It would be her last delivery before nightfall.

This continued throughout the early nesting period, no matter how long his work day, despite all other concerns. The last to leave the limited world of the birdhouse continued to seek him out. And he continued to assist in protecting and tending to its needs until it was able, on its own, to join mama bird among the tree branches.

It was a blessing to witness, from a distance, this silent commitment. It was humbling, moving, revealing. It's been said that character can be defined by what one does... when no one is watching. How loving, how tender... that heart.

He and "Blue" continue on with their evening connection: A climb up the pant leg to perch on a shoulder, alighting upon his head to sit awhile, hide-and-seek among the rocks near the river. It's true, man and bird enjoying each other's company, as mama bird looks on, never far away.

Lists

Do astronauts have lists? Do they carry pen and pad to jot down some of the most important things they need to remember? How about jet pilots or doctors? I have many lists. There's the list for tomorrow, the one for today, leftovers from yesterday's list that get transferred. There's the summer list, the accomplish before winter list, and yes, the winter list. On the fridge is the ongoing "up north" list, with little checks by what's ready to go. It accompanies me there to be added to as thoughts occur for the next trip.

One morning, while wondering if others remember to water their plants without putting it in writing, I paused. Was it possible to accomplish the requirements of the day without looking at a piece of paper? Closing my eyes, I visualized the kitchen table, the pen, the pad of paper. Zooming in on that first item there on the notepad, I imagined myself standing there, pen in hand, ready to cross off whatever that might be and move on to the next item. No use! I could not make it out without my glasses. Sinking down into my favorite chair, it hit me hard: I am list dependent, an addict to written stimuli.

Without lists, the grass would grow beyond mower manageability and bills would pile up until services were disconnected. Upcoming events would pass by, remembered as "I could've gone" occasions. Without lists, my train would pull into the station each night minus a few cars.

I read somewhere, once, a long time ago, that it's best for the memory to work out ways to remember by using the association of things, little mind triggers. Not anything like tying a string around a finger. Now, what good would that do, unless you needed to be reminded to tie something up, like maybe the hollyhocks needed support? The association idea made sense at the time, but the details of how it works are in the closet of my mind somewhere, in the dark, because I didn't write it down. There is not a switch to turn that light on.

Important appointments are always written on the calendar, but are also noted on the list, lest I forget to look at that monthly planner page. A lost list can lead to irritability, mild anxiety, and yes, even sleeplessness. What's a chronic lister to do? I plan to wean myself from this overdependence during the winter season. Lists are shorter then. The list will be placed under something so as not to be so obvious, in hopes of honing my memory skills. Just knowing it's still available will prevent unnecessary panic. I'll just leave a note on the fridge to remind me where the list is.

Crackdown?

With the "crackdown" period (drunken driving) now behind us, will it be back to statistics as usual? Such measures no doubt do save lives and hopefully leave a lasting impression on some offenders. Yet, as the weekly news informs us, it does not on others.

Our state: number one in the entire country for driver intoxication. Shame on us! Could we not, should we not rise to that outrageous challenge in a more forceful and consistent manner? What hope is there for significant and lasting change when we tolerate the unacceptable? We could drop to the bottom of that list and create a mighty wave of justice across the nation.

Operating a motor vehicle is a privilege. For some, it may need to be permanently denied. If we continue to focus on reducing, rather than eliminating repeat offenses, we are but applying bandages, without antiseptic, to an oozing, gaping wound.

The very first offense for drunken driving calls for a penalty severe enough to make a lasting impact. A fine far greater than presently enforced, as well as mandatory involvement in drunken driving prevention is not at all unreasonable. Viewing footage of accident scenes and intoxicated individuals would be a great requirement during jail time, as would visits with victims of offenders, their families and friends. I would be the first to volunteer.

Recently, on a news program, was a most insightful report. Professional race car drivers were each given two shots of liquor, then proceeded to drive an obstacle course. They were astounded to discover that they could not get through without knocking down pylons. Professional drivers! Everyone needs to know that.

A drunken driver took the life of both my young son and my dearest friend, who were in the vehicle I was driving. The physical injuries and scars are the least of what is carried on. It was 34 years ago this past Labor Day weekend. He came from behind, over a hill, at approximately 95 mph. He felt no pain. He was not injured. He did not even realize what he had done.

Photos taken of a vehicle after such an impact would provide quite somber and sobering reflection. No one seeing such photos would believe one could have survived. It is a miracle that I did… a miracle, and a tragedy.

Jason

My son, I love you beyond
Means of expression known to me
Yet, I feel the buds my mind contains
Blossom... in some distant Garden
Where the fragrance of each unfolding petal
Calls out to you
In a language only spirit comprehends

"Gripper"

You are thought of
When the gray and misty dawn
Becomes alive with shimmering strips of gold

Reaching… ever reaching
You are with me, dancing among the leaves
Falling softly, riding gently, on the breeze
We laughed together

The waves come to greet us
Hand in hand we greet them
Oh joyous tears… we cried together
Moments we have shared, on my mind…
You are thought of

Realm Divine

In Heaven, is there humor
Amongst the angels
Within the realms of Light where spirits soar?
Do we leave behind us here on earth the laughter
Or expansively embrace it so much more?

Are weary souls who've left this world now smiling
Those who seldom smiled in this life?
Freed now from all burdens that were carried
No longer weighted down by grief and strife

In Heaven, are departed ones now dancing
To melodies we here are yet to know?
Although in prayerful silence we can sense them
Subtle rhythms through us gently flow

Memories within the mind are carried
Beyond existence of the human brain
Unrestricted by the earthbound garment
No doubt a broader vision we shall gain

From Heaven, gems of wonder rain upon us
Loving showers for all upon the Earth
Yet, heedless do we scurry and toil, unmindful
Of our journey toward a second birth

In Heaven, is there humor? I believe so
For in this life our laughter is a sign
Of what awaits us ever more intensely
Within a Realm, embraced by the Divine

END

"Created, to seek out all Truth
And strive for connections of hearts
To nourish, and tend to our souls
To heal what keeps us apart"